HIDDEN HISTORY *of* ELKO COUNTY

HIDDEN HISTORY *of* ELKO COUNTY

Claudia Wines

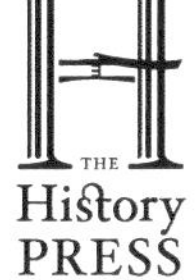

Published by The History Press
Charleston, SC
www.historypress.net

Front cover: courtesy of Northeastern Nevada Museum.
Back cover, top: courtesy of Northeastern Nevada Museum; *bottom*: courtesy of Northeastern Nevada Museum.

First published 2017

Manufactured in the United States

ISBN 9781626199958

Library of Congress Control Number: 2016945809

Contents

Contents

Acknowledgements

Many thanks to those hardy souls who were the history of Elko County. It was a rugged land, and life was not easy. They struggled through hard winters, dry summers and long, hard traveling to civilization. Those who live here now appreciate the perseverance of our early settlers.

My thanks to those who have researched and written about the history of Elko County, either one story or a whole book. They have all done their part to preserve our history.

Also, my thanks to Toni Mendive and Thad Ballard, for always helping me find just the right picture.

Last, but not least, I appreciate my family: my late husband, Gordon, who shared my love of local history; and my children, Gretchen, Ira and Margaret, who spent countless hours on the phone hearing about this book, and Catherine, who proofread it and made creative suggestions, which made it much better. My thanks to my late parents, Harvey and Margaret Dahl, who settled in Starr Valley when I was four years old and started my lifelong love affair with Elko County.

To all of these, I owe a debt of gratitude.

I

Leona Reynolds

Was It Billy Graham?

Leona Kimmerle Reynolds spent thirteen of her eighty-eight years in the small town of Currie, in southern Elko County. Not many other people lived there; it was in the middle of nowhere. The nearest town was Ely, Nevada, seventy-five miles away. There was one thing that made life pleasant for the inhabitants, and that was the railroad. In Nevada at that time, most small towns' only connection to civilization was by horse and buggy on a dirt road.

Leona's story began in Putnam, Ohio, in 1886. During her school years, she had a teacher named Earl Reynolds. He tired of teaching, moved to Nevada and got a job with the newly built Nevada Northern Railway. This ran north from Ely to Cobre, some 125 miles, where it joined the transcontinental Central Pacific Railroad, constructed in 1869, from the Pacific Coast to the Mississippi River. Earl's first position with the railroad involved opening a new telegraph office and railroad station at Currie. But before he began, he returned to Ohio and married his former student, Leona, in 1908.

The newlyweds took all their belongings and a month's worth of groceries and rode the train to Currie. Their home was in the railway depot; so began many exciting events for the new bride.

She immediately fell in love with the country around Currie. She had a friendly, outgoing personality and soon had many friends. There were only a few people living there at the time, but she became acquainted with most of those who lived on surrounding ranches.

Leona told of trips to these ranches for picnics and parties. The Goshute Caves were twenty miles from Currie, and she and her friends would go there by horse and buggy. They loved crawling through low, narrow openings and admiring the stalactites that almost met the stalagmites among the beautiful pools of cool water.

In addition to the railway depot, there was a hotel in Currie, and finally, as more people moved to town, there arose a need for a school. The State of Nevada required a minimum of eleven students in order to establish a school, but there were only nine children in Currie. The state would not relent, so one of the nearby ranchers hired a family that had two children. The entire community pitched in to help build a schoolhouse, which also served as a community center and space for dances, parties, election boards and any other necessary functions.

There was no store in town, so after a few years of saving their money, Earl and Leona decided to start one. They ordered supplies, which arrived on the train, and soon it was a huge success. In addition to the townspeople, ranchers from as far away as seventy miles and nearby Indian tribes frequented their store. They soon expanded from just food to clothes, fabric and sewing supplies, machinery, hay, oats and anything else that the local people needed. The store kept them so busy that Earl finally quit his job with the railroad and devoted all of his time to the mercantile.

Leona told many tales of dealing with rattlesnakes. She saw one nearly every time she stepped out her back door. In an attempt to lessen the number of snakes in town, the men found a nearby rattlesnake den and dynamited it, which helped somewhat. Jackrabbits were also a problem, as there were hundreds of them around the area. The railroad ran a special train to Currie from Ely every Sunday carrying more than one hundred people, who would spend the day shooting rabbits to try to help thin them out.

The Reynoldses' store was so successful that they eventually could afford to build their own house. They also constructed a chicken coop, and Leona started raising chickens and selling eggs, which added to the profitability of the store.

The Italian man who ran the hotel in town married a girl from Italy, who spoke no English. Leona and several other women in town included her in all their jaunts around the countryside; although they could not converse, she enjoyed their friendship. Later, when the newcomer was expecting a baby, her husband planned to take her to Ely, the nearest hospital. The baby decided to come early, and Leona was called on to be a midwife. It was a successful experience, and she consequently delivered a number of babies

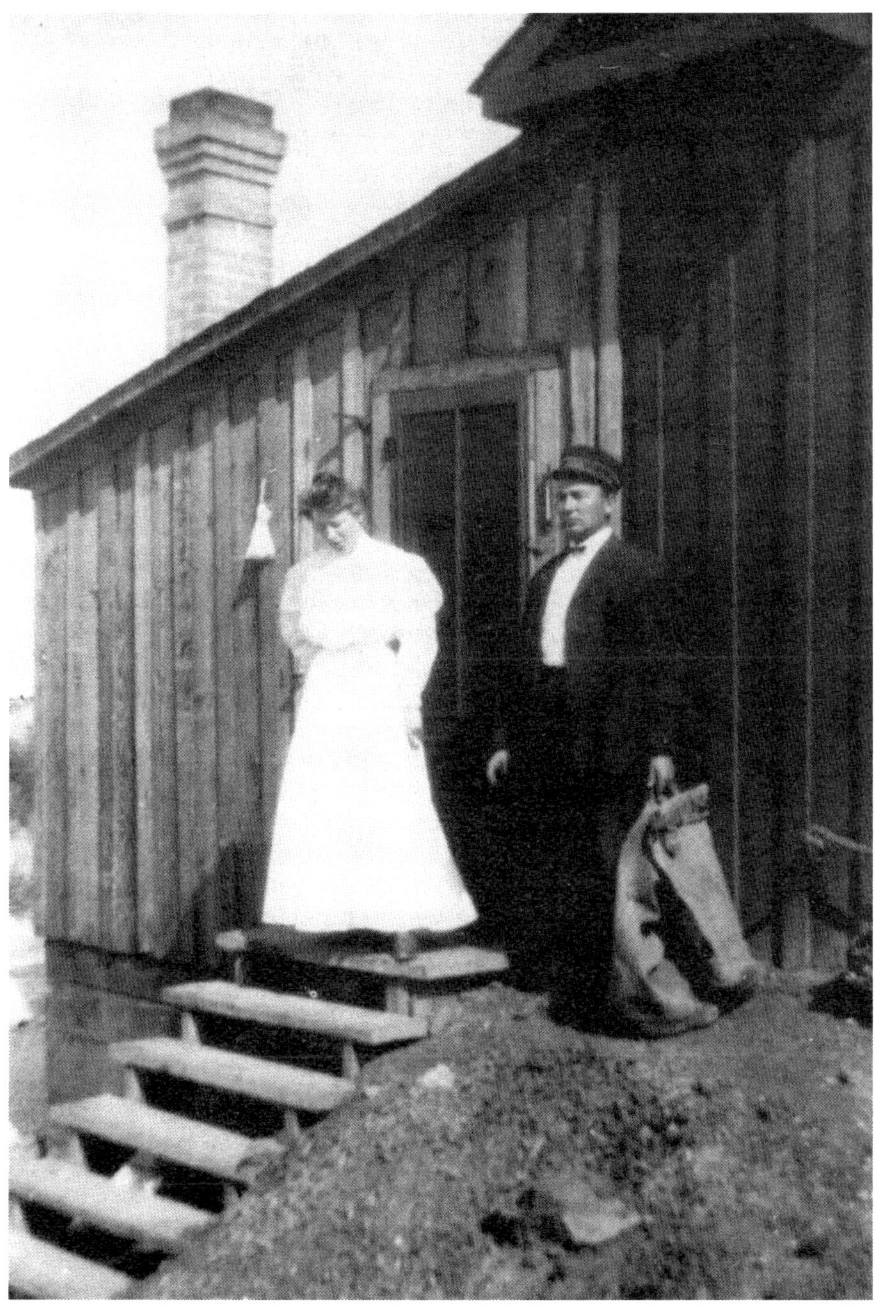

Leona and Earl Reynolds in front of their first house in Currie. *Courtesy of Northeastern Nevada Museum.*

through the years. She also served as a mortician when someone died, until an undertaker could make the trip from Ely to Currie.

When Leona looked back on her life, years later, she had many tales to tell about the time spent in Currie, but the most exciting thing that stuck in her mind was the day Billy Graham came to town—twice. He didn't actually come to Currie; he just passed through, but he was in an automobile, probably the first to go through Currie, and it provided something to talk about for years to come. If it was, indeed, Billy Graham, it was probably William Graham Sr., the father of the well-known evangelist.

This happened one day when a couple arrived in Currie in a brand-new Buick. Many people in Currie had never seen a car. The road, which was only a dirt trail used by horses and wagons, was not conducive to automobile traffic. Billy Graham was driving, and his wife was in the back. They stopped in Currie for a few minutes before speeding off down the road. They made it part way to Wells when they ran into a herd of cattle and hit one of the cows. The collision tore the top off the car and threw the animal into the back seat, on top of Mrs. Graham. She was not seriously injured but decided she'd had enough of automobiles. She caught a ride into Wells with the mail stage, boarded the train and returned home. Mr. Graham drove the topless car back to Currie, sold it to Earl Reynolds for $250 and then he, too, caught the train home.

Earl and several of his friends spent many hours working on the Buick, and the Reynoldses and their friends enjoyed it for years.

The Reynoldses had two children, and in 1921 the family moved to Elko, so the children had more opportunities at school. They spent twenty-one years living there and in 1942 moved to Reno. Earl died in 1957, and Leona died in 1974, at age eighty-eight. They had many fond memories of Currie—especially all the fun they had in Billy Graham's Buick.

2

THE O'NEIL FAMILY

Bad Neighbors

An article in the *Elko Independent* newspaper of November 13, 1887, had this to say about the O'Neil family: "Their phenomenal increase of worldly possessions on the ranges of the county has been marked by a corresponding loss from the herds of neighboring cattlemen."

Richard C. "R.C." O'Neil, the father of this redheaded wild bunch, traveled to California during the gold rush but was only there a short while. He and his Irish wife, Mary, had two sons, R.C. Jr. "Dick" and William "W.T."; after spending a short time in California, they moved to Virginia City, Nevada. There a daughter, Mary Alice, was born, and the family moved again, this time to Hamilton, White Pine County, in east-central Nevada. They again moved to Spring Valley, to the east of Hamilton, and took up ranching. The 1880 census lists three more children, James "J.P.," Eva and Charles.

Their first trouble with the law in White Pine County happened in 1883. A neighboring rancher, William Bassett, caught the O'Neils putting some of his horses in their corral. He confronted them, and they let him take back his horses, but they threatened him. Several days later, three men, hiding on a hill above him, shot Bassett. He was severely wounded but lived long enough to tell what had happened. Lawmen from the nearby town of Osceola arrested R.C. and his two oldest sons and held them in the local jail. Several weeks later, in the middle of the night, a hooded mob broke into the jail and started shooting. They killed R.C. and wounded Dick and W.T. The local citizens were shocked at the act of shooting defenseless, sleeping men, but no one tried very hard to find the culprits or bring them to justice. The local newspaper, *White Pine News*, editorialized that the O'Neils were bad neighbors, and they had terrorized many people since they moved to Spring Valley. Their shooting of Bassett was the final straw, and though no one condoned the mob trying to get rid of the O'Neils in that manner, it was doubtful a jury could be seated in White Pine County to indict those who had killed R.C. O'Neil. The newspaper editor was right, and no one was ever charged with his murder.

Officials also feared they could not impanel an impartial jury in White Pine County to try the case of the O'Neils for the murder of William Bassett, so they moved the trial to Elko County. The trial lasted for a week, and the cost of providing transportation and lodging for everyone involved made it very expensive for White Pine County. It was the middle of winter, and a huge snowstorm during the trial made the return trip to White Pine very difficult, requiring another week. The jury, knowing of the O'Neils' reputation and fearing for their lives, declared them not guilty. None of this made the residents of Spring Valley any fonder of the O'Neils.

Realizing they had used up their good luck, the O'Neils immediately packed up and left White Pine County. People thought they went to Idaho, but they actually only got as far as northern Elko County, where they began ranching again. The editor of the *White Pine News* wrote on June 7, 1884, "The O'Neils have skipped the country, bag and baggage....They have beat everyone who had anything to do with them, friends and enemies alike. The general verdict is that the county has got rid of a bad crew."

The family immediately started causing problems in their new home, and Dick and W.T. were soon accused of stealing a neighbor's cattle. The deputy sheriff in nearby Wells arrested them and was in the process of locking them in the local jail when a man stepped out from behind a nearby building and fired at the brothers with a shotgun. Neither of them was hurt, but their sister, Alice, who was nearby, got into the middle of it and was wounded in the ankle. The O'Neil brothers escaped but were later caught and taken to jail in Elko. They each paid a $2,500 bond and returned to the ranch, but they neglected to show up for their trial. Several deputies rode out to the O'Neils' ranch and tried to arrest them again but were met by the entire family, armed and ready to fight, so the lawmen returned to Wells empty-handed. The next day, the O'Neil brothers rode into Wells, armed to the teeth. W.T. O'Neil shot at the sheriff, who finally managed to arrest them, and they all headed for the jail again. The same stranger who had shot at them earlier arrived on the scene, as did Alice with more guns. The O'Neil brothers escaped again and ran to a nearby house, where they barricaded themselves. They were finally arrested and taken to jail in Elko again.

It's not known if the stranger was really trying to shoot them or if he was part of their plot to gain sympathy and thus avoid being convicted. Both stories have come to be part of the lore of the Old West and were told in an article about Elko County in *Life* magazine in 1949. The jury feared for their lives, knowing of the O'Neils' reputation, and acquitted them. They agreed to leave the county, but they did not.

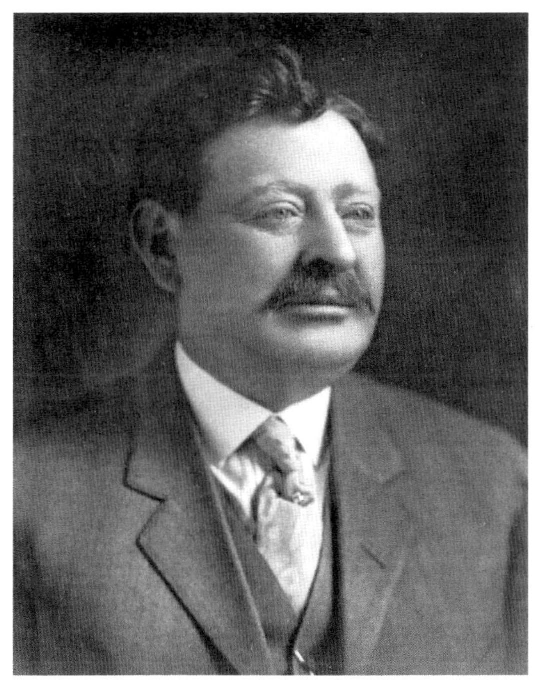

James "J.P." O'Neil, one of the notorious O'Neil brothers. *Courtesy of Northeastern Nevada Museum.*

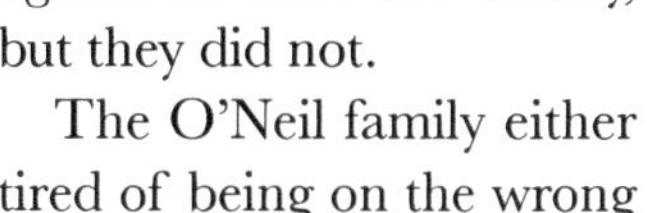

The O'Neil family either tired of being on the wrong side of the law or they managed not to get caught; they seemed to settle down after that. They expanded their ranches and, in 1925, were one of the largest sheep and cattle producers in the state of Nevada. However, they always retained a reputation for being difficult to deal with.

In 1925, a downturn in cattle and sheep prices forced them into foreclosure, and they lost all their ranches. They each went their separate ways and started other enterprises. In later years, as they each died, they were remembered in their obituaries as good, decent people who were astute businessmen, so apparently they developed a degree of respectability in their old age—or just didn't get caught. The area in northern Elko County where their ranches were located is still known as the O'Neil Basin.

3

Joe Harris

Cow Shoes

In the late 1920s, workers of the large UC Ranch in northeastern Elko County noticed cattle disappearing. There were never more than a few at a time over a several-month period, but everyone was at a loss to explain it. They never found horse or human footprints near the herds. One day, some buckaroos rode over a hill and noticed a man walking behind several head of cattle. It was J.R. Hazelwood, better known as Crazy Tex. He worked occasionally on area ranches, but most people would not hire him because of his bad reputation. As they approached him, they noticed two strange contraptions on his feet. He had taken cow hooves, fastened them to two boards and put straps over the top. He wore them on his feet, so the only footprints resembled those made by cattle. The ranch owner called Elko County sheriff Joe Harris, and Crazy Tex spent the next several years in prison.

Joseph Crawford Harris, Elko County sheriff for twenty-six years, was born in Fort Collins, Colorado, in 1878. It was ironic that he would become a much-respected sheriff. Joe's father, Tom Thumb Harris, grew up in Cedarville, California, and in 1873, at age twenty-three, shot and killed a man. Instead of facing years in prison, he and his new wife, Libby, fled the state and settled in Colorado. While living there, hiding from the law, their first child, Joe, was born. Seven years after the murder, a judge in Cedarville determined it was self-defense and pardoned Tom.

Tom moved his family to Huntington Valley, south of Elko, when Joe was two years old.

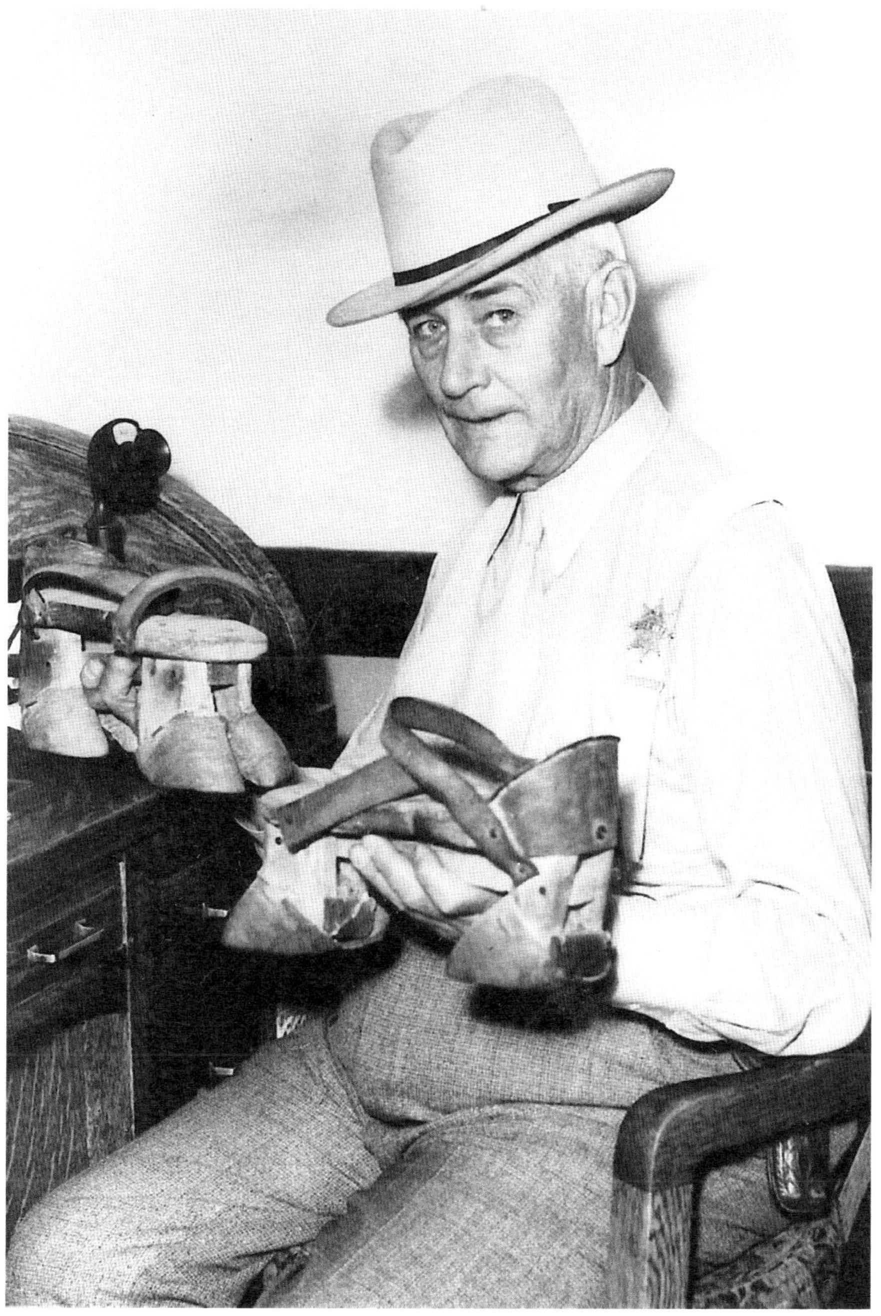

Sheriff Joe Harris at his desk, holding the cow shoes that Crazy Tex used to rustle the neighbors' cattle. *Courtesy of Northeastern Nevada Museum.*

Joe and his three siblings attended school in the valley and then Elko High School. When the Spanish-American War broke out in 1898, Joe enlisted in the army in a volunteer cavalry unit. The group was sent to Camp Cuba Libre in Florida, where they languished for months, waiting to go into action. The living conditions were bad, and many men contracted typhoid fever. When the war ended, a total of two hundred men had been killed in action and twenty-five hundred had died of various diseases. Joe and his group were mustered out and sent home. They never left Florida and never fired a shot.

Joe was elected Elko County sheriff in 1910. The area covered seventeen thousand square miles, larger than many states. He traveled by horseback, buggy or train to carry out his duties in rural areas.

One occurrence happened in Jarbidge, a remote mining camp in northern Elko County only accessible in winter by going north into Idaho and then turning back south on a dirt road to Jarbidge. In December 1916, Ben Kuhl murdered the mail stage driver near Jarbidge, and Joe was summoned. He traveled to Odgen, Utah, then north to Pocatello, Idaho, and west to Twin Falls, Idaho, all by train. Then he caught the horse-drawn mail stage to Jarbidge. It took three days. This was the last known robbery of a horse-drawn stage in the United States. Sheriff Harris found a letter in the snow near the crime scene with a bloody palm print on it. The print belonged to Kuhl, and the sheriff presented it during the trial. Fingerprints had been used as evidence for years, but this was the first instance in the country in which a palm print was used. Kuhl was convicted and served twenty-eight years in the state penitentiary in Carson City, Nevada.

Joe Harris was well known and very well respected all over the West. He was offered the position as warden of the state prison in Carson City, and Reno officials asked him to be their chief of police. He turned down both jobs. He said he wanted to stay in Elko, where he knew everybody by their first name. He never lost an election; very few times did anyone even run against him.

During his time in Elko, G.S. Garcia, the famous saddle maker and metal craftsman, made a badge for Sheriff Harris. It was of solid gold from the nearby Tuscarora gold mines. Joe had spent a great deal of time in Tuscarora through the years, solving problems, and the appreciative citizens donated the gold for the badge. The inscription on the badge read "J.C. Harris, Sheriff, Elko County, Elko, Nevada." Joe wore it proudly for many years. His son Jess Harris followed in his father's footsteps and later served as Elko County sheriff for twenty-nine years. Because their initials were the same, Jess also wore the gold badge during his years as sheriff.

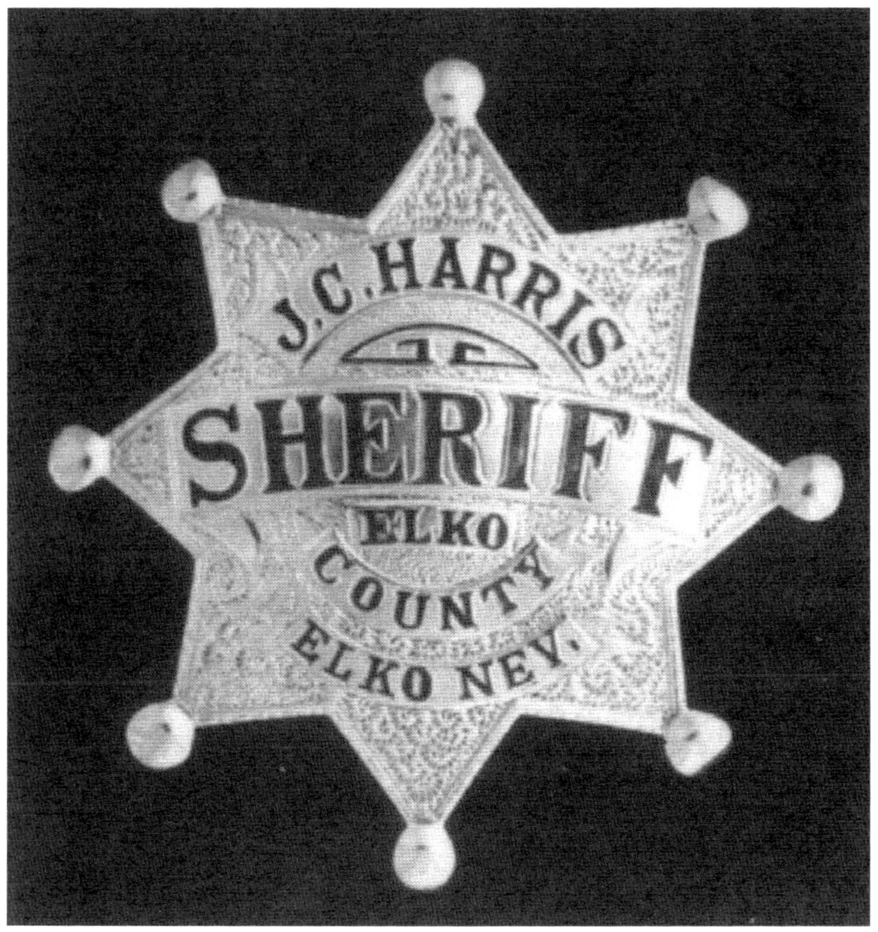

Gold badge crafted by silversmith G.S. Garcia and worn by both Joe and Jess Harris. *Courtesy of Northeastern Nevada Museum.*

Joe, always tough but fair, had many friends. The stories of his exploits through the years could fill a book. John Oldham later told one of these stories, about when he was a youngster. He recounted:

> [A friend and I] *used to go to the grocery store every Sunday and buy a package of bacon and some bread. We'd walk out to Yeates Canyon, build a sagebrush fire, and cook lunch. We always took a couple of guns to shoot rabbits or ground squirrels. One afternoon, we shot a few telephone insulators off the telephone line—pretty good targets for two boys, you know. 'Course, the next morning, there wasn't any telephone service.*

Sheriff Harris saw the young man in town on Monday and asked him what he'd been up to over the weekend. John said he'd been with a friend and shot two boxes of shells at squirrels.

"You didn't shoot any insulators, did you?" Joe asked.

"Yes, sir, we did," John replied. "We didn't shoot the ones that go up to Tuscarora. We only shot two altogether. I don't think I'll ever shoot another one, though."

"Well," cautioned the sheriff, "I hope you don't."

As the sheriff walked away, John asked, "Where you goin', Mr. Harris?"

Joe smiled. "I'm goin' looking for them guys that shot them insulators." Neither of them ever mentioned the incident again.

Another time, two boys were playing in a boxcar in Salt Lake City, Utah, and their friends locked them inside just as the westbound train moved away. Joe was notified, and he met the train in Elko. He took the two scared, crying little boys off the train and drove them back to Salt Lake City, rather than wait for their parents to come and pick them up.

After all his close encounters in gunfights and dangerous situations, Sheriff Joe Harris died in 1936 of uremic poisoning after a bout with pneumonia. All the county offices, most stores in town and even the U.S. Post Office closed for his funeral.

Through the years, Sheriff Harris gathered up an assortment of pistols, blackjacks, brass knuckles, knives and numerous rifles, many valuable antiques among them. Some had been used during the Civil War. There were also swords worn by soldiers at nearby Fort Halleck and opium pipes used by the Chinese population in Elko. Years later, Joe's family donated this valuable collection, including the gold badge, to the Northeastern Nevada Museum, where it is on display in the history gallery. Crazy Tex's cow shoes are front and center.

4

Margaret Taylor Wines

Park and Parcel

Margaret Taylor Wines spent a good part of her life in remote Ruby Valley, Elko County, in the latter half of the nineteenth century, but she had some interesting experiences elsewhere.

To start with, she was born Margaret Taylor in 1846 in Hollenwood, Oldham, Lancashire, England. She was one of fifteen children. When she was two years old, the family made a very rough boat ride across the choppy Atlantic Ocean. Eventually, they ended up in St. Louis. When she was seven years old, the family crossed the plains with a group of pioneers and settled in Lehi, Utah Territory. She saw an infant brother die and buried on the plains.

Meanwhile, in Terre Haute, Indiana, Ira Doty Wines II was born in 1844. He was the youngest of six boys, and his father died when he was only one month old. His father, Ira Doty Wines, had been a successful businessman and left his widow very well off. Three of the six boys died at an early age. In 1850, when young Ira was six years old, his mother, Jane Maria Shearer Wines, with help from her father and two older sons, drove a team and wagon across the plains. They also settled in Lehi, Utah Territory.

Ira D. grew up in Lehi but at a young age went to Ruby Valley, Nevada. He worked on ranches near where the Pony Express and Overland Stage went through. He was too big to be a regular Pony Express rider but would fill in occasionally when needed. He also drove the Overland Stage under similar circumstances.

In 1865, Ira returned to Lehi and married Margaret Taylor. He was twenty-one and she was nineteen. They moved to Ruby Valley, where by

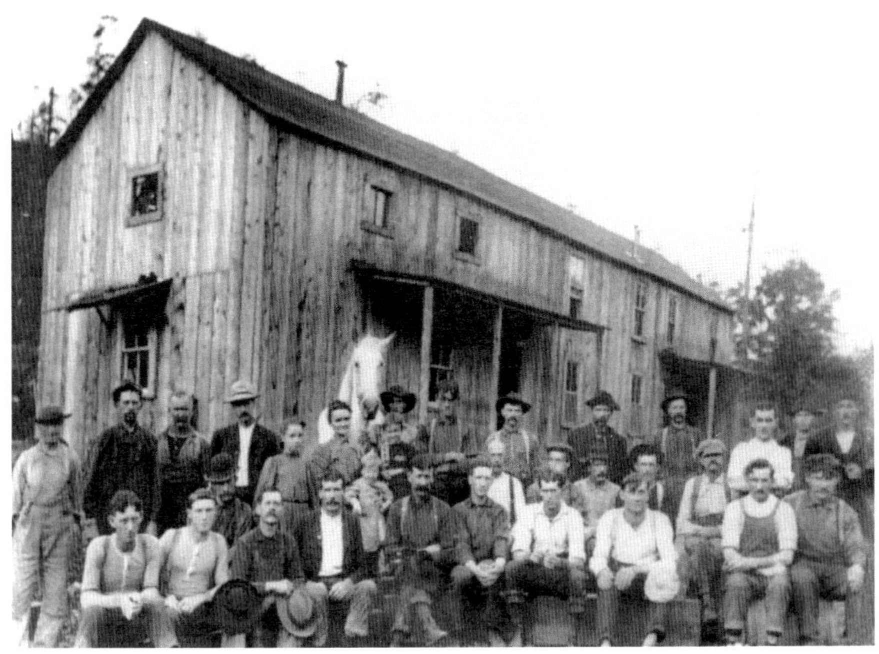

The neighbors gathered for a picture in front of the grain mill on the Overland Ranch, owned by Ira D. and Margaret Wines. *Courtesy of Northeastern Nevada Museum.*

now he owned the Overland Ranch. They would have twelve children, but only seven would grow to adulthood. Ira built a home on the property he still had in Lehi, and Margaret would spend a great deal of time there for several reasons. Good medical help was available there when she had her babies, and as the children got to school age, the education facilities were better in Lehi.

In 1892, when her youngest child was a year old, Margaret moved back to Ruby Valley to stay. The family went on the train to Halleck and then by team and wagon nearly fifty miles south to the Overland Ranch. Two of the older sons brought the furniture and household equipment by teams and wagons across the desert from Lehi to Ruby Valley. The trip took them two weeks.

By then, Ira had established a flour mill, a general merchandise store and the local mail route. The mail came from Halleck three times a week, going out one day and returning the next. Freight lines would haul flour and grain to many areas, and local ranchers would come to his store once or twice a year for supplies. The Overland Ranch was a busy place.

A Chinese cook on the ranch also did the washing and ironing. He chopped wood for the fires, cut up the meat after slaughter, fed the pigs

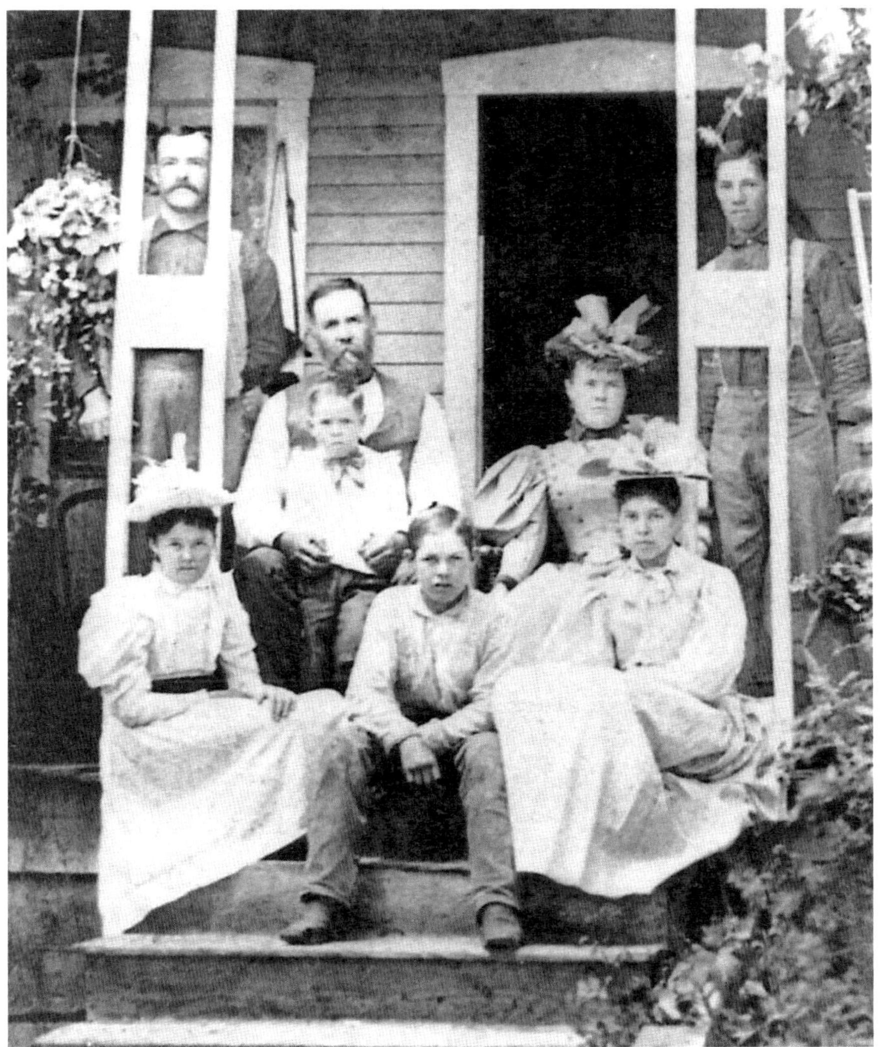

Margaret and Ira D. Wines with six of their twelve children on the porch of their house on the Overland Ranch in 1894. *Courtesy of author's collection.*

and raised a garden. The younger girls milked the cows. In the summers, during haying, three tables would be set up for eating. The women and children would eat first, and then the large hay crew. The Indians on the crew would eat at a table outside. There was no indoor plumbing, and all the water used in the house was carried in buckets from a nearby creek. Hot water came from a reservoir attached to the back of the wood-burning stove and from teakettles.

From the grain raised on the ranch, they would fill all the beds in the house with new straw each fall after threshing. The first few nights, many family members would fall out of bed. It took several nights to make a dent that fit their bodies so they would not roll off the rounded heap of straw.

The younger children attended a one-room school near the ranch. They traveled in a one-horse cart or on horseback.

Ira did not discipline the kids—Margaret did. She used a willow switch kept behind a framed picture. When it broke, she would send one of the children to bring another.

Margaret's health deteriorated; in her later years, she, Ira and their two youngest children spent winters in San Francisco. In the spring of 1906, Ira and their youngest son, Blaine, returned to the ranch. Margaret was still in poor health, so she and her daughter Florence, age twenty-two, stayed on in California. On April 18, the Great San Francisco Earthquake happened. They were on the fifth floor of a hotel and were fortunate that falling chunks of ceiling plaster did not hit and injure them. Outside, they watched in horror as everything in the city seemed to be on fire and the shaking continued. They went to another hotel but soon had to leave there, too. Eventually, Florence was allowed to return to their original room to collect their belongings. Several men helped her get the trunks to a safe place; much later, the trunks were sent to Nevada on the train. Margaret and Florence spent several weeks in a park in Oakland with nothing but a few clothes and blankets from the hotel to sleep on.

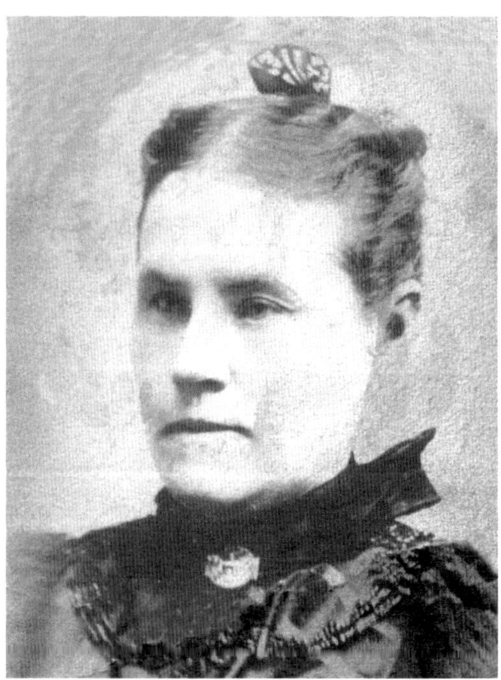

Margaret Taylor Wines. *Courtesy of author's collection.*

The family in Ruby Valley knew of the earthquake, and Ira and another son, Stanley, went to San Francisco on the train to try to find them. They never did connect, but the family members were finally all reunited in Halleck as the two trains they traveled home on arrived, one shortly after the other.

Margaret died two years later, at age sixty-two, in Palo Alto, California, where she had again gone because of failing health. Ira would live another fifteen years.

The acreage where Ira and Margaret's house in Lehi had been located was donated to the city for a park and named the Margaret Wines Park. It retained that name for many years. In the 1980s, the city fathers, thinking no one knew who Margaret Wines was, planned to rename the park. A granddaughter-in-law, Lourinda Wines, heard of this. She traveled to Lehi with a list of hundreds of descendants, most from Elko County, and explained the history to them. It is still named Margaret Wines Park.

5

Domingo and Gregoria Sabala

Home Sweet Home

Domingo and Gregoria Sabala were two of the many successful immigrants to come to the United States from the Basque country. While most started out as sheepherders, working on ranches or cooking in Basque hotels, many eventually became successful businesspeople and contributed a great deal to their communities. A few of them established hotels, bars and restaurants, which served as places for other Basques to gather in the new country. Domingo Sabala, usually known as Dan, and his wife, Gregoria, took that route, establishing the Overland Hotel in Elko.

Domingo was born in 1881 in Gizaburuaga, Vizcaya, a Basque province in the Pyrenees Mountains in northern Spain. At the age of nineteen, he came to America, seeking his fortune, and never returned to his native land. From the East Coast, he traveled across the country by train and landed first in Winnemucca, where he worked on ranches.

Gregoria Garties was also born in Vizcaya, Spain, in 1881, and she traveled to America in 1904 to join her sister, who was already living in Winnemucca. She and Domingo were married three years later and moved to Elko.

The next year, the Sabalas built their dream, a hotel in downtown Elko. It was the second-largest Basque hotel in the city at the time. It was three stories high, but the height was its biggest dimension. It was on a very narrow lot, across Fourth Street from the Commercial Hotel and across the alley behind where the Tabor Building and Henderson Bank Building were erected several years later. The ground floor was originally a handball court, a game popular with the Basque people. The next floor included a

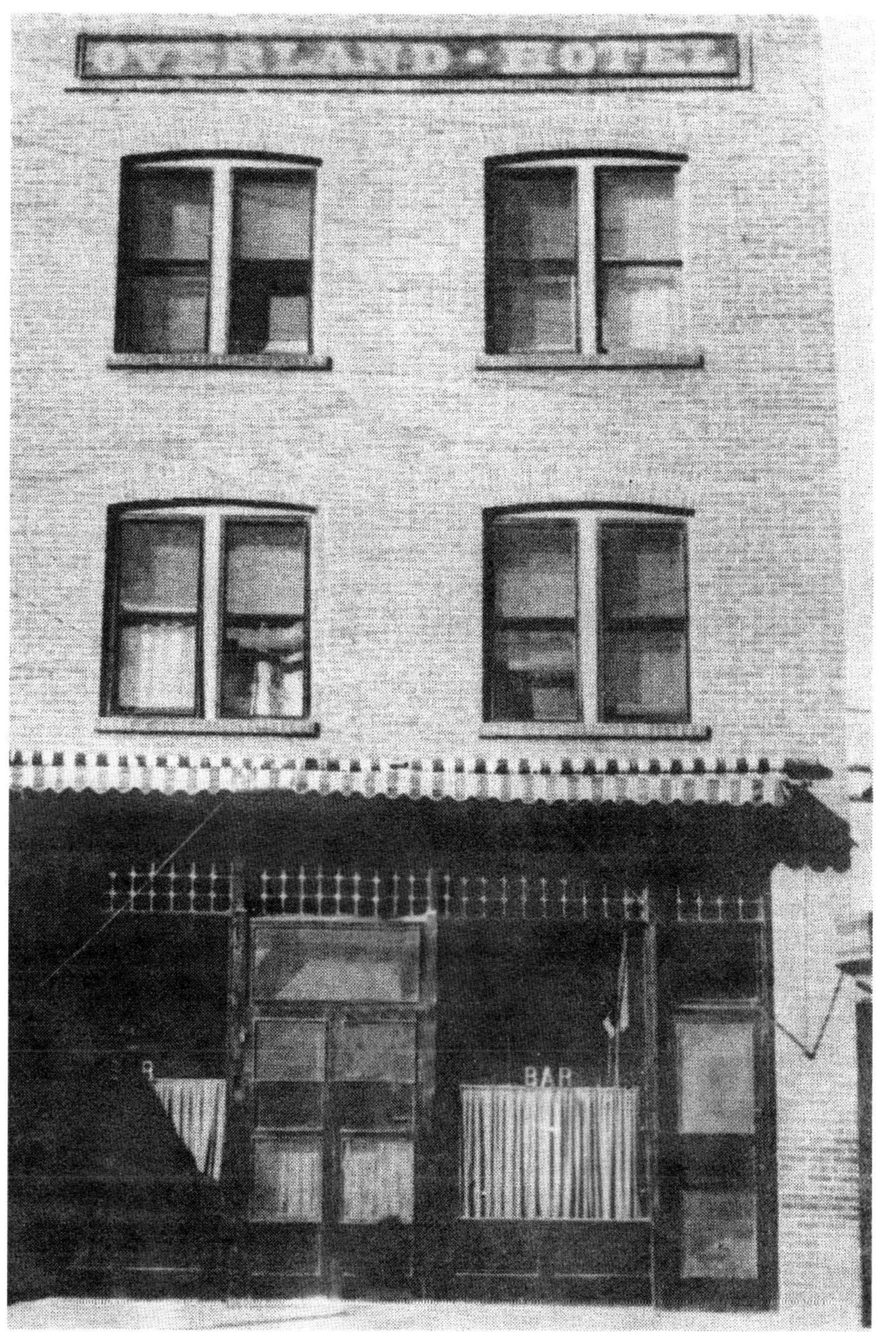

The Overland Hotel, owned by the Sabala family. *Courtesy of Northeastern Nevada Museum.*

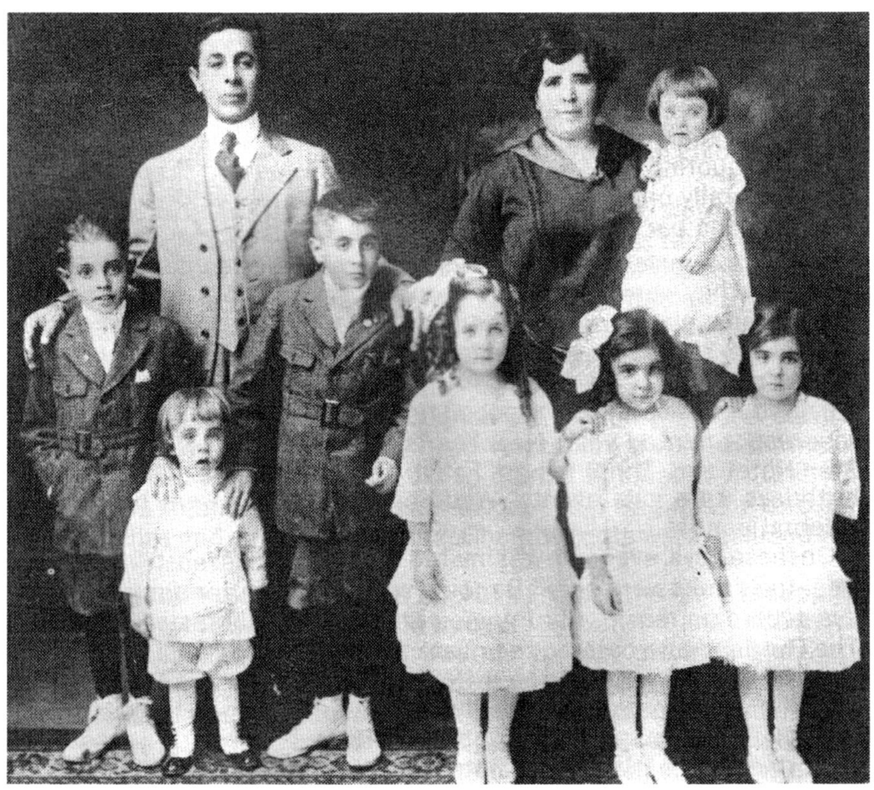

Domingo and Gregoria Sabala and family. *Courtesy of Northeastern Nevada Museum.*

dining room, kitchen, bar, lobby, cigar counter and maintenance rooms. The top floor consisted of twenty-four rooms, some of them used by the Sabala family for living quarters; the rest they rented out.

The Overland was a home base for the many young Basque men who came to Nevada to herd sheep. It was a good place to find work; Gregoria mothered them and helped them adjust to their new life. She helped with the language; most only spoke Basque when they arrived. Since many sheepherders sold their flocks in the fall, a number of the young men did not work during the winter and would live at the Overland, waiting for spring. They had a comfortable room and meals in the restaurant, which always served Basque food, reminding them of home. Some had no money to pay, but the Sabalas trusted them to pay after they went back to work and were seldom disappointed in their generosity.

A number of young Basque women came to the area and worked in the hotel as maids and cooks. Many ended up marrying the men who frequented the hotel.

In those days, with very few modern conveniences, running a hotel required a lot of work. The linens were washed once a week in a hotel bathtub, using a washboard. Iceboxes kept food cold, as the hotel had no refrigeration. Ice came from icehouses in Carlin, delivered once a week. A dairy in Lamoille delivered milk. On nearby land, the Sabalas had a large vegetable garden and raised lamb and beef, all of which contributed to the dining at the hotel.

The Sabalas used wood stoves in the building for cooking and heating water for bathing and laundry. A coal furnace in the basement, with steam heat, kept the building warm. Light was supplied by kerosene lamps, candles or whale oil lanterns, and each room had a chamber pot.

As time went on, the hotel became more modern. An electric washing machine lightened the laundry load, electric lights replaced kerosene lanterns throughout the building and chamber pots gave way to pull-chain water closets.

Rooms at the hotel were reasonably priced and included meals. Drinks at the bar were a real bargain and indicative of a drinker's habit. A person could have ten drinks for a dollar. As was customary at the time, and still in force many years later, women were not welcome in the bar.

The Overland Hotel and the Star Hotel, the other Basque establishment in Elko, were centers for holiday celebrations and social events. Weddings, birthday parties and even wakes happened in these hotels. There was only a small Catholic church in Elko at this time, so weddings, confirmations and baptisms were often held in the lobby of the hotel. With no mortuary in town, many of the Catholic faith had rosaries at the hotel, and occasionally, bodies lay in state there before the funeral.

During Prohibition, through a discreet entrance in the alley, drinking continued. The hotel was part of a vast network of illegal drinking places, and word went from one establishment to the next when government agents were on their way, so the evidence disappeared. The milkman from Lamoille often brought alcohol to town in milk cans, along with the milk.

Through necessity, Gregoria became a midwife and delivered many babies in the upper rooms of the Overland Hotel. During the influenza epidemic that coincided with World War I, the Overland's rooms and halls were often overflowing with patients lovingly nursed back to health by Gregoria. She never lost one. Domingo was a community leader and always willing to help people in need. He became one of the most respected and successful Basques in Elko.

The story of Domingo and Gregoria doesn't end happily, however. The Great Depression hit; along with most of their neighbors, they lost everything.

Domingo, at fifty-seven years of age, went from a successful businessman to a bartender, railroad worker and janitor.

The Overland Hotel went through several owners and uses and was razed in the 1950s. The land on which it stood is now a parking lot. Domingo and Gregoria's dreams of success in America flourished before they were eventually dashed. Gregoria died in 1952, at age seventy-one, and Domingo in 1954, at age seventy-three, but the people of Elko County fondly remembered the Sabalas for their kindness throughout the community for many years.

6

Henry Harris

Almost a Slave

He started his life in Texas, the son of former slaves, and ended life as one of the most well-respected cowboys (known locally as buckaroos) on a large ranch in northeastern Nevada.

Henry Harris, the oldest of twelve children, was born in Georgetown, Williamson County, Texas. Conceived in slavery, he was born free in 1865, shortly after the Civil War ended. He received some schooling and was able to read and write.

At a young age, he went to work as a houseboy for a local rancher, John Sparks. When Henry was seventeen, his boss organized a large cattle drive to northeastern Elko County in Nevada, to a ranch he had acquired there. Henry went along on this drive, still assisting with domestic duties.

John Sparks had several partners through the years, and this cattle empire, known first as Sparks and Tinnin and then Sparks and Harrell, stretched from Wells on the south to Twin Falls, Idaho, on the north, east to the Utah border and west to the Bruneau River. The ranch ran between fifty thousand and seventy-five thousand head of cattle.

In Nevada, Henry still stayed at the home place, but Sparks noticed his keen interest in horses, cattle and the buckaroos who worked with them. Henry expressed an interest in being a buckaroo. Thinking the novelty would soon wear off, Sparks let Henry try the life of a cowboy. He proved an apt student, and Sparks finally realized he could not be denied. Sparks sent to Texas for another houseboy. It wasn't long before others realized Henry was one of the best.

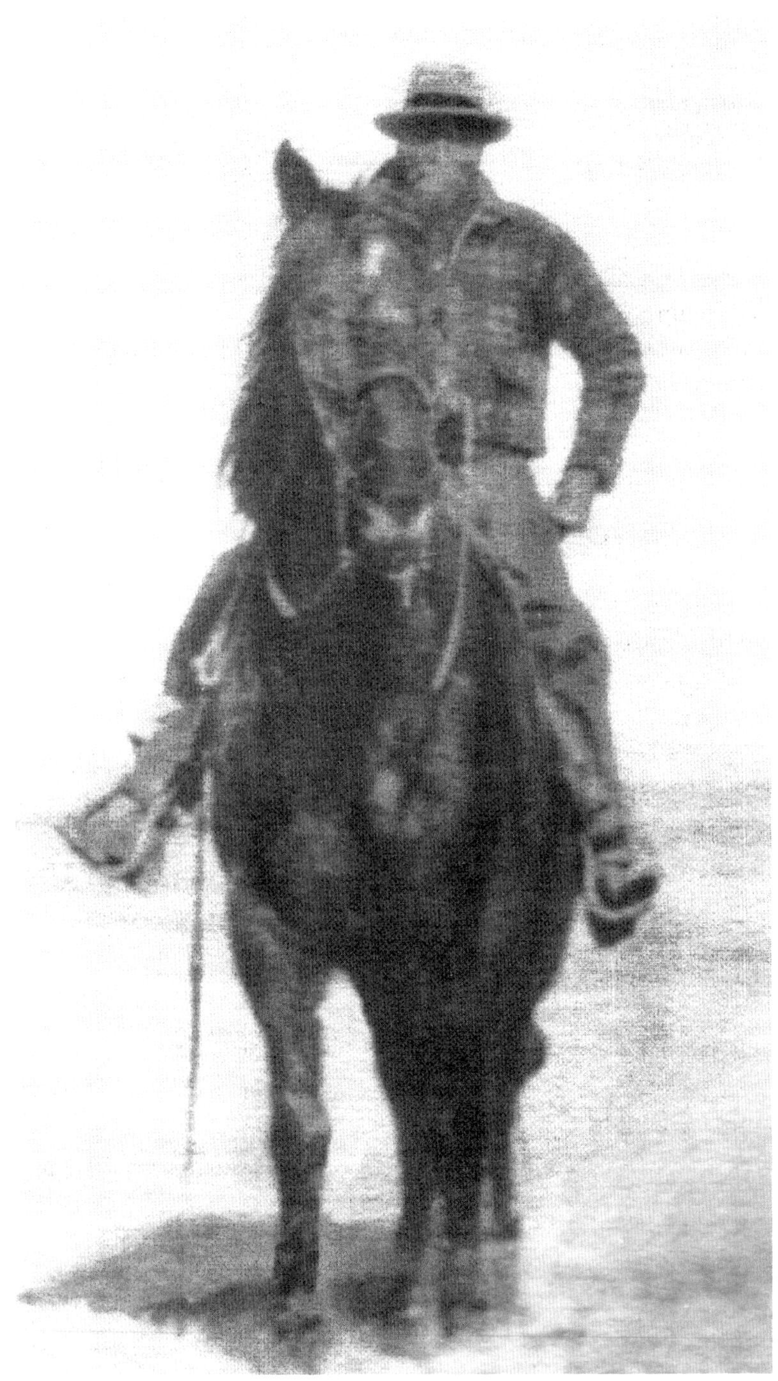

Henry Harris. *Courtesy of Les Sweeney.*

John Sparks became the tenth governor of Nevada in 1903 and sold his ranching interests in Elko County. He moved to Reno and Carson City, and Henry remained on the ranch, working for each new owner through the years. He became foreman of a buckaroo crew, referred to as the Vineyard Wagon. This important position was granted to only the best cowboys, and many were shocked when Henry took over the job. But he soon proved equal to the task.

The large Utah Construction Company, known locally as the UC, bought the ranch in 1913, and Archie Bowman, a prominent cattleman, became the general manager. Both Archie and his wife, Nora, were very fond of Henry. Years later, Nora Linger Bowman wrote a book, *Only the Mountains Remain*, about the thirty-two years the Bowmans spent on the ranch. In this book, she told many stories about Henry and his exploits. In language typical of the time but considered insensitive today, Nora wrote about Henry's death, saying, "Our faithful, much-loved Nigger Henry passed away….It is with no disrespect that I call him Nigger Henry, for it was so that he was known throughout the state. He knew we all liked and respected him and that he was welcome wherever he went." The word did not have the same connotation that it has today.

A number of "colored cowboys" came from Texas and worked for Henry through the years. Historian Les Sweeney, who has done extensive research on this era, told that in the days when Henry was running the Vineyard Wagon, Negroes and whites were not considered equal throughout most of the country and that Henry had been raised this way back in Texas. When his outfit was working by themselves, the whites and Negroes sat down to eat together, but if a stranger came around the wagon, Henry would tell him to help himself but never got a plate and made sure that none of the other colored cowboys did, either, until later, unless the stranger indicated it was all right.

Sweeney also described an occasion when the Utah Construction Company people were in Boise, Idaho, at a court hearing regarding water rights. The group decided, at the conclusion of the trial, to go downtown and have a drink. Henry had testified at the hearing and was one of the group. They went in several bars, but Henry was not welcome, so they would leave and go to another one until they found an establishment that would serve him. However, when they got ready to leave, the bartender broke the glass Henry had been drinking from.

According to the U.S. government census, in 1900 there were only 134 blacks in the entire state of Nevada, and 7 of them worked for Sparks and

Harrell on the large ranch they owned. These included Henry and 3 of his brothers, who had come to Elko County to work for him. The census-taker must have had a sense of humor. He listed Henry as head of the household and his brothers and the white men on his crew as servants.

Henry never married. He said that there weren't a lot of black girls running around in the sagebrush in Nevada.

Through the years, Henry adopted many of the traditions of the early California vaqueros with his dress and gear. Author Adelaid Haws, in her book *The Valley of Tall Grass*, describes buckaroo dress of the time. She referred to them as "those gay vaqueros, of silver mounted saddles and bridles with Spanish bits, of bright shirts and big, red silk handkerchiefs, of long tapaderos [covers on stirrups], silver mounted spurs, rawhide reatas [lasso ropes] that would reach sixty to seventy feet, and fancy boots with high heels."

Archie Bowman always admired Henry's cowboy skills. He once said, "Henry Harris could ride anything with hair on it."

Because he was so well respected, Henry was called on several times to testify in legal trials. On one of these occasions, in 1897, two sheepherders were murdered in the area. Jack Davis, better known as Diamondfield Jack, a disliked man in the area, was charged with this crime. Most people were determined to see him convicted. Henry testified at the trial that Davis did not do it, but the general feelings prevailed, and the jury sentenced Davis to hang for the crime. Before he was executed, another local man, Jeff Gray, confessed that he had done it. Henry said later that he knew Gray did it, because Gray had told him he had killed the sheepherders. When people asked Henry why he hadn't revealed this at the trial, he answered that no one had asked him, and since Davis didn't do it, he didn't expect he

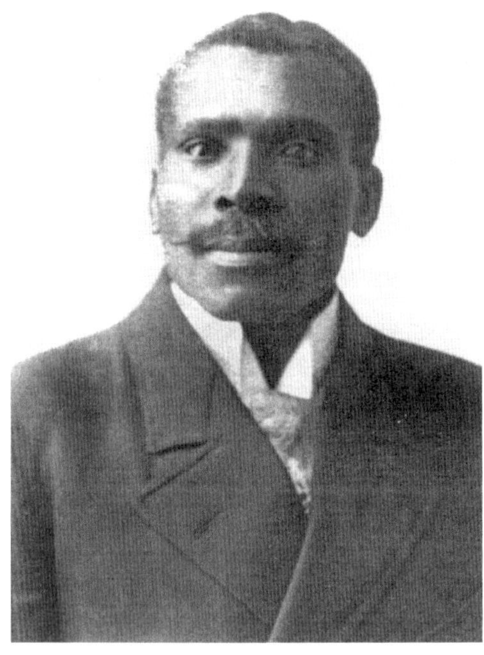

Henry Harris had this portrait done in Twin Falls, Idaho, to send home to his mother in Texas. *Courtesy of Les Sweeney.*

would be convicted. Henry's statement proved true, and Diamondfield Jack was released.

One of the railroad stations on the Oregon Short Line Railroad that ran between Wells and Twin Falls from 1909 until 1978 was named Henry, after Henry Harris.

Henry died in 1937 at the age of sixty-nine and is buried in the Twin Falls, Idaho cemetery. Cowboys still talk about the legend of Henry Harris, an accomplished buckaroo with a reputation for being able to ride horses many others could not and for being a good man to work for. At a time and place that produced many fine buckaroos, Henry Harris is remembered as one of the best.

7

Harry Cazier

He Turned the Lights On

To the people of Wells and Starr Valley, Harry Cazier was just another kid who grew up on his father's ranch, graduated from Wells High School and went off to college in Reno. He went way up in their estimation in 1927 and became a local hero.

Harry was born in 1885. Shortly after his birth, his father bought a ranch about eight miles west of Wells. Like the rest of rural Elko County, there was no electricity, at least none that was pleasant to use. Some folks had diesel generators; they were noisy, expensive and only supplied DC power. And only a few things could operate at a time—lights or the washing machine or the refrigerator. Elko, forty-five miles to the west, had fairly reliable electricity in the early 1900s because of a power plant on the creek in Lamoille Canyon. A line from there ran twenty-five miles into Elko. Nobody else in the county had electric power, only generators.

Harry went to college at the University of Nevada. He majored in engineering, and at the beginning of his senior year, the university offered a new program: electrical engineering. He was the first student to sign up. He graduated with an electrical engineering degree in 1906. While living in Reno, he enjoyed the benefits of reliable AC power, but when he went home to visit, he faced reality; most of Elko County still lived in the "dark ages."

After Harry graduated from college, looking for adventure, he spent two years in the wilds of Central America, employed as an electrical engineer, and enjoyed living on the edge. He loved his adventures but eventually decided he should go home and help his father on the ranch.

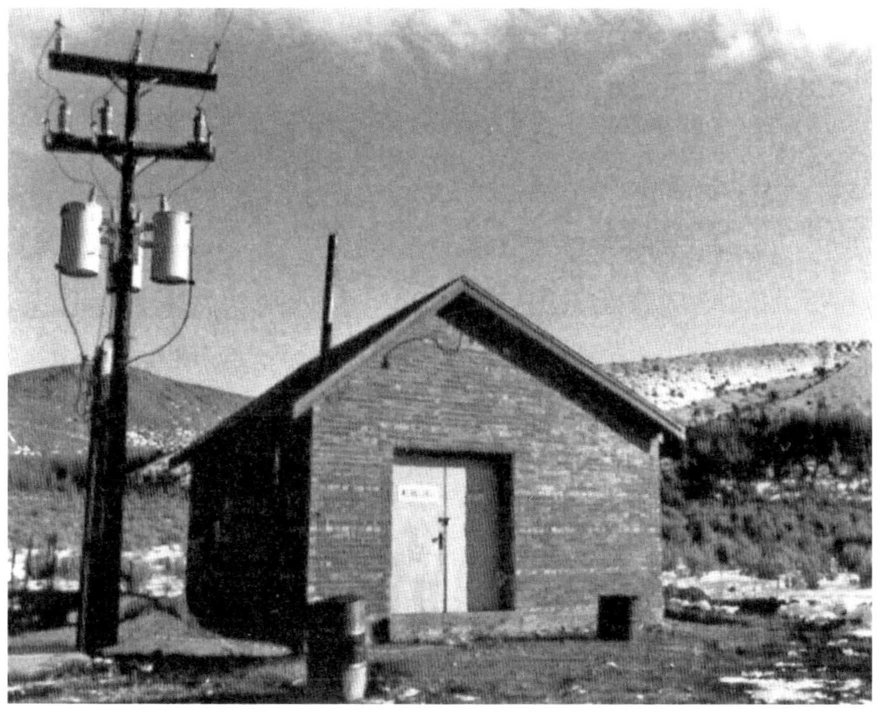

Current picture of the Hydro, where Harry Cazier established his first power source. It's still in use. *Courtesy of Wells Rural Electric Company.*

He began lobbying the businessmen in Wells to invest in a study to see if Trout Creek, a stream on his dad's ranch that had its source in the nearby Ruby Mountains, was sufficient to run a power plant. It took him more than twenty years, but in 1926, the study was completed and determined the project to be feasible. Harry went to work and built the first fully automated hydroelectric plant in Nevada, a few miles from the ranch headquarters. In 1927, lines were strung and Wells and nearby Starr Valley had electricity. There were 115 homes in Wells and 30 businesses connected to the lines, as were most of the ranches in Starr Valley. Moving into the present century, Wells installed streetlights. It cost $132 per month to keep them lit. Total cost of the entire project, for equipment, pipeline, building and distribution lines, was $40,250.

Nearby ranches in Ruby Valley, Clover Valley and Metropolis continued to use generators for the next thirty-one years and were envious of their neighbors in Starr Valley. In 1958, a group formed the Wells Rural Electric Company, a local co-op, which was part of the

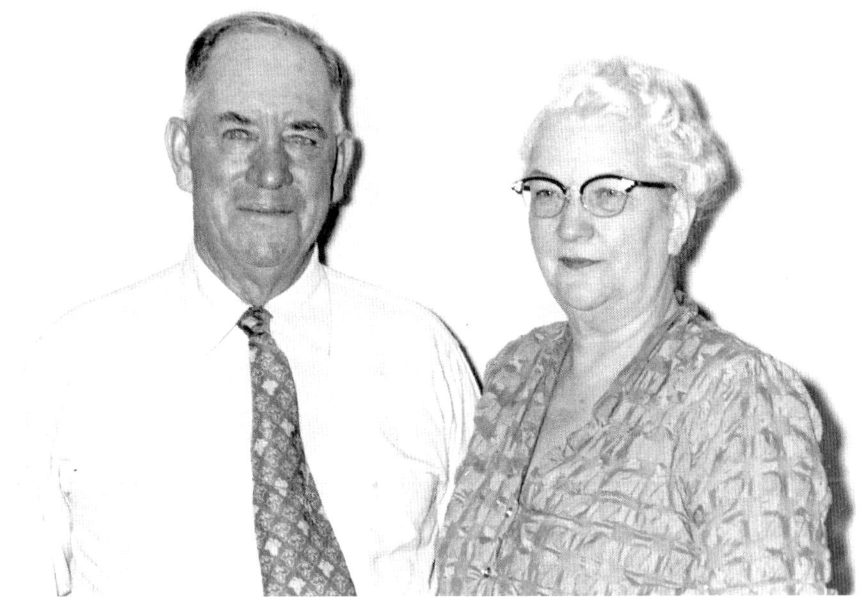

Harry and Neva Cazier. *Courtesy of Wells Rural Electric Company. Anita Cory, photographer.*

Rural Electrification Act of the federal government, and the rest of the surrounding area finally had electricity.

Wells Rural Electric Company now furnishes power to many parts of Elko County, but it still maintains the little power plant that Harry built on Trout Creek. It has been lovingly cared for by a number of employees, most notably Gene Supp, who dedicated forty-eight years—his entire working career—to the power plant. It currently produces about seven hundred thousand kilowatts a year. Called "the Hydro," it just keeps chugging along.

Harry took over the family ranch after his father was gone. He married a neighbor, Neva Dewar, and they had four children.

The year after his hydro began producing electricity, and always thinking of new ideas, he decided Trout Creek could also sustain a fish hatchery. In 1928, he established the first one in Elko County. It served the area until a larger one, still in operation, was located in Ruby Valley.

Always community minded, he served as president of the Nevada Monarch Mining company at Spruce Mountain, fifty miles south of his ranch, for twenty-seven years. Harry was one of the founders of the Elko County Cattle Association, which became Nevada Cattlemen's Association, still in existence today, representing the ranchers of Nevada. He was a member of the Elko County School Board and served as a director of the Wells Chamber of Commerce for many years.

After Harry retired from the ranching business, two of his daughters and their husbands, Harriet and Dennis Procter and Catherine and John Blecka, took over the management of the ranch. They remained an integral part of the local community for many years, until the ranch sold in the 1960s.

Harry died in 1963 at the age of eighty-one. With all the important things he did in his life, what his neighbors appreciated the most was the day they got electricity.

8

Kate St. Clair

Service in the Face of Adversity

Those who knew her marveled at this remarkable woman and wondered where she received the strength to survive the many tragedies that befell her—and how she managed to keep a good attitude through it all.

She was born Mary Kate Reed in Springdale, Arkansas, in 1891. Some of her strength came from the example of her mother, a remarkable woman herself. Kate's father died when she was thirteen, and her mother raised seven children by herself, seeing to it that they all received at least some college education.

Kate spent a year at the University of Arkansas, planning to become a teacher. After a year of school, she traveled to Nevada to visit relatives and remained to teach a year at Rabbit Creek School in Pleasant Valley, near Lamoille. After spending another year studying in Arkansas, she returned to Nevada and taught at North Starr School in Starr Valley. A beautiful young woman, she was courted by Arthur St. Clair, a very intelligent son of a local rancher. Arthur had already made a name for himself in the area. While at the University of Nevada in Reno, in 1911, he became Nevada's first Rhodes Scholar at the University of Oxford in England. There, he not only excelled at his studies, but he was also an outstanding athlete on the school's rugby team.

Arthur and Kate were married and spent their honeymoon camping in the nearby Ruby Mountains, making the trip on horseback. Instead of Arthur pursuing his education, the couple moved to nearby Deeth. He became the bookkeeper for the Union Land and Cattle Company, a large firm with headquarters in Deeth and ranches in both Nevada and California. He also served as the town constable, similar to a sheriff, and Kate ran the post office. They had two sons, Reed and Jim. Tragedy struck when Jim, age two, drowned in an irrigation ditch.

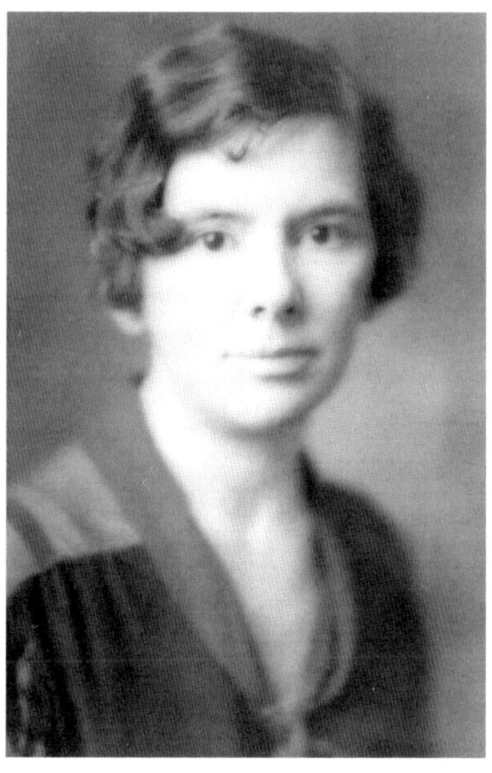
Mary Kate Reed at the time she married Arthur St. Clair. *Courtesy of Northeastern Nevada Museum.*

The couple had been married for five and a half years when a band of robbers held up some businesses in Elko and headed out of town. Arthur joined the posse to capture them. Near Cherry Creek in nearby White Pine County, the posse caught up with the robbers. In the shootout that followed, Arthur was killed. The couple's third son, Arthur, named after his father, was born five months later. Kate and her two young sons went back to Arkansas, where she continued her education, ultimately receiving a bachelor's degree in education.

A few years later, she returned to Elko County and taught in Montello for a year and then in Elko. The tragedies in her life were not over. Her son Reed, who was as smart as his father, was a freshman at the University of Nevada and resented having to take many of the freshman classes, feeling he already knew those subjects. He also thought physical education and ROTC were unnecessary. He became despondent and committed suicide in 1934, at age twenty.

Kate continued to teach in Elko until 1944, when she received an appointment as state deputy superintendent of public instruction. She was in charge of forty-five schools, forty-two of which were in rural areas. She spent a great deal of her time traveling to visit each of these schools. She had to use her own vehicle, for which she received five cents per mile as compensation. Her salary was $2,700 a year.

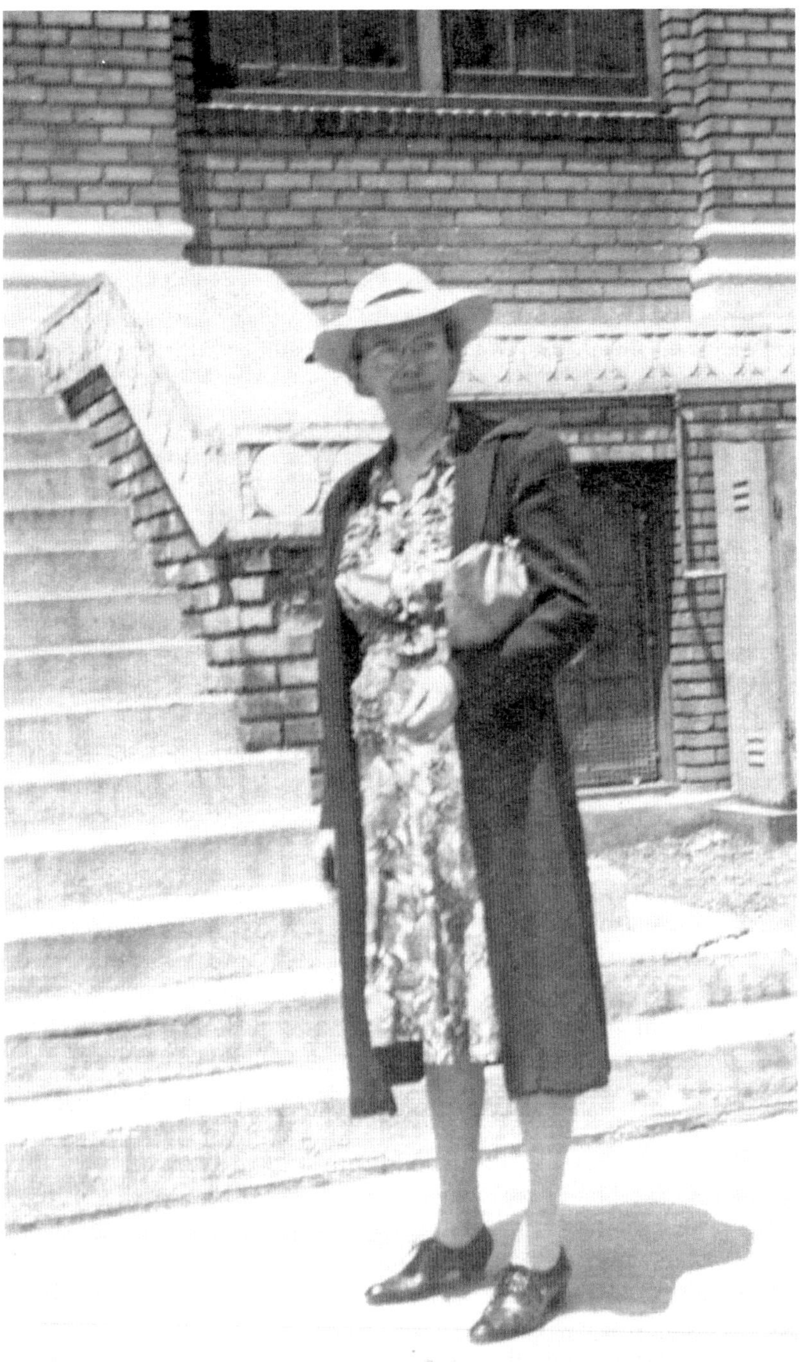

Kate St. Clair in front of a school when she was the state deputy superintendent of public instruction. *Courtesy of Northeastern Nevada Museum.*

More sorrow was visited on her. Her youngest son, Arthur, working with the Red Cross, was accused of embezzling funds from that organization. He was never formally charged, but he became despondent and turned to alcohol. Several years later, he contracted cancer and died at age forty-two.

After serving as the state deputy superintendent of public instruction, a title Kate always thought a bit pretentious, she retired after fifteen years on the job, at the age of sixty-nine. The publisher of the *Elko Independent*, a local newspaper, wrote the following about Kate:

> *Unfortunately the time must come when officials of her cut and pattern must retire. There will be no statue erected in the public square in recognition of her service to humanity. School teachers and administrators seldom win fame to be marked by material evidence. But for many a year a fond memory will remain of her and her effort to bring education to rural Nevada.*

Kate kept busy in her retirement. She traveled extensively, visiting forty-eight states, Canada and Mexico. She helped establish a Senior Citizen Center in Elko, and in 1971, Nevada governor Mike O'Callaghan appointed her as part of the Nevada delegation to the White House Conference on the Aged. She enjoyed life thoroughly, in spite of all the sorrows that had befallen her family. The editor of the *Elko Independent* said this about her retirement years:

> *Kate St. Clair was a fine example of what old age should be. She accepted retirement from the field of education only as a means of making way for other activities. She was fortunate in having the kind of health that permitted her to participate in various community activities, particularly those related to the aged.*

Kate died while traveling with relatives in Yellowstone Park in 1973, at age eighty-two. She was remembered for her great inner strength and her ability to elevate herself above and beyond tragedy. She always felt the best way to deal with her sorrows was to serve others.

9

Pete Itcaina

An Unlikely Millionaire

Pete Itcaina was rich, but it's a hard story to believe, because he was not very careful with his money. A sheep and cattle rancher, he acquired a small fortune in his lifetime, in spite of his careless ways.

A French Basque, Pete Itcaina (pronounced It-china) was born in Aldudes, France, in 1880. When he was old enough to be drafted into the army, he chose to go to America instead. After several bad business ventures, he bought some land at Stag Hill, seventeen miles south of Charleston in northern Elko County, and finally found his niche, raising sheep and cattle. He became a citizen in 1910, which was an easy process at that time.

He married Augustina Zozaya, a Basque girl who was a cook at the Telescope Hotel in Elko. She was a happy-go-lucky person who counterbalanced his grouchy, ornery disposition. For the first few years of their marriage, they lived in a small cabin that had once been a barn on the stage line from Deeth to Jarbidge. It had no running water, electricity or indoor plumbing. Most ranches did have at least some modern conveniences by then.

Pete bought another ranch near the Mary's River, one in the O'Neil Basin and one near Currie. He acquired forty thousand acres from the Central Pacific Railroad between Deeth and North Fork and ran approximately twenty thousand sheep and two thousand cattle.

Pete never cleaned up to go to town. He always wore bib overalls and a dirty shirt, and his long, droopy mustache was burned on the ends from his carelessness with roll-your-own smokes.

He was never careful with his money. He would not cash checks, because he didn't want to pay taxes on them, always putting his taxes off until the next year. Once, he lost his wallet on the road to Charleston, and a hay hauler later found it. There was a check for nearly $30,000 in it. When the man gave the wallet to Pete, he refused to take it, saying it was not his. Because it had his name on it, he finally had to admit it belonged to him, and he grabbed it and stomped off, cursing the hay hauler.

Augustina tried to keep track of his money for him, but it was not easy.

Celso Madarieta, a well-respected and knowledgeable local livestock buyer, purchased most of the sheep and wool in northeastern Nevada, including the Itcaina livestock each year. Pete once received a check from Celso for more than $100,000, put it in the toolbox in his truck and forgot about it. Months later, he discovered it, all torn and greasy, and had to take it back to Madarieta for a new one. He never cashed another check from the same source for $20,000, and the IRS decided to collect taxes from Madarieta for the amount. Pete said he had already cashed it, but Augustina found it in an overall pocket, all torn and falling apart.

The tax collectors finally caught up with Pete and determined that he owed more than $1 million in back taxes. He never kept records, so he went to Reno, where he and his lawyer negotiated a settlement with the IRS of $200,000, and he wrote them a check. The government later determined it had made a mistake and refunded him $46,000. There is no record of what he did with that check.

Pete was in town one day, dirty and disheveled, and went into the Silver Dollar Bar for a drink. The bartender, thinking he was a bum who had no money, wouldn't serve him. Pete went in the back, found the owner, bought the bar and went out and fired the bartender. He then bought drinks for the house. The next day, after he calmed down, he rehired the bartender and leased the establishment back to him.

Many times when he went to town and had too much to drink, he would fall asleep in his truck in the middle of the street. Everyone knew him, and the law didn't prosecute him for those indiscretions. One day, he was driving the wrong way down Commercial Street—it was a one-way street—and he plowed into a friend of his and completely destroyed the man's car. As the aggrieved man got out to yell about it, Pete rolled down his window and roared, "Let's go have a drink, friend."

An acquaintance of Pete's, Aleck Tourreuil, was helping put up hay at one of Pete's ranches. Aleck was running a buck rake on a new tractor and got it stuck in the mud. He walked to the house, and he and Pete returned to the field to pull the tractor out. Aleck wanted to drive the truck, but Pete insisted. Even though Aleck reminded him to drive slowly, he gunned the truck and took off with a jerk. The new tractor broke in half. Pete just took off his hat and slapped himself on the head.

Pete had a very generous side that was not well known. He often loaned money to people in need and never charged interest when they repaid him.

As Pete got older and his wife's health deteriorated, he sold his ranches in 1957 for nearly $1 million and moved to Elko. He died two years later, at the age of seventy-nine. The couple had no children. One would hope that whoever ended up with his money was a little more careful with it than he was.

10

Austin Peltier

The Man Who Could See with His Hands

How could a blind person be a telephone operator—especially in the days before automation? An operator was everyone's sole connection to the outside world, spending the entire work shift at a switchboard, taking incoming calls, connecting outgoing calls and dispensing all sorts of information. Everyone depended on the local telephone operator, and the thought of a blind person doing this was not only unheard of, it was easily dismissed. Austin Peltier proved it was not only possible but actually quite easy.

Austin was born in 1899 in Deeth. His father was a rancher, and Austin worked as a cowboy on local ranches. At age twenty-two, he married Julia Wiseman, granddaughter of one of the early settlers of Clover Valley. Two years later, a horse kicked him in the face, and he lost his sight permanently. One of the local newspapers, the *Elko Independent*, published this short news article:

> *Austin Peltier, well-known resident of the eastern section of the county, was quite seriously injured yesterday on the Bob Steele ranch in Clover Valley. One of the government stallions on the place became unmanageable and in seeking to avoid the horse, Mr. Peltier fell and the stallion immediately whirled and kicked him squarely in the face. The injured man had to crawl through the corral and into the ranch house where he telephoned for assistance. He was brought down* [to Elko] *on No. 1* [train] *last evening and taken to the hospital, where he lies in a serious condition.*

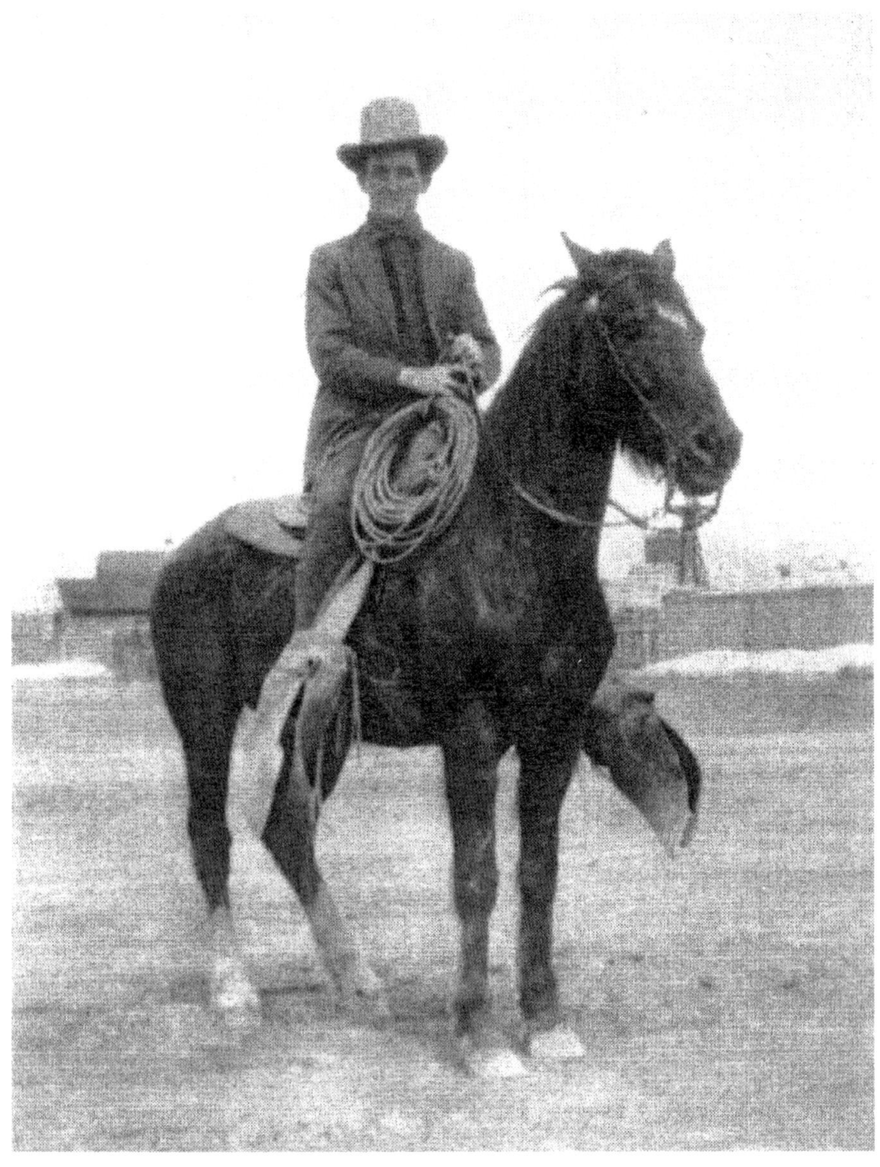

Austin Peltier, shortly before an accident that cost him his sight. *Courtesy of Northeastern Nevada Museum.*

> *He suffered a great loss of blood and his face is all broken out of shape, his nose smashed and one eye completely gone. He is suffering a great deal, but everything is being done to relieve his condition and it is to be hoped that he pulls through.*

He was later treated in specialized hospitals in Salt Lake City and California but had so injured a nerve that the best eye specialists told him he would never see again. Years later, he commented that he thought that, with modern technology, doctors could have saved the sight in one eye. He added that he had no regrets and had learned to live without sight. "I can go everywhere and get around," he said. "There's worse things than being blind."

After a couple of years, he went to work for the telephone company in nearby Wells as an operator, a job he would have for the next thirty-eight years. He handled the switchboard entirely by feel, serving the greater part of eastern Elko County.

He was a favorite of all the citizens of Wells and the surrounding area. Always friendly, he never let his handicap dampen his disposition or his sense of humor. One winter day, when the temperature was below zero, he told a friend that when he put the coffee pot on that morning, the coffee boiled in the middle and froze around the edges.

He was the local information bureau. He kept track of the stock market, and cattle buyers would call him, trying to locate cattle for sale. He always had the correct time when called. He knew who was in town at any given minute, why they were there and how long they would be there. He ran an informal employment service, became a telephone repairman and served as the tourist information bureau. He helped out at home, washing dishes, dusting and sweeping, and was considered an excellent cook

Austin had a remarkable memory, never forgetting a name, a voice or a phone number. He was a great asset to the local police and fire departments. A switch in his office turned on a red light at the police station, and a large siren, installed outside his telephone office, would summon the volunteer firefighters. He took special care with calls from soldiers when they called home during wartime. These always took priority so that the soldiers could be assured a chance to talk to their families.

During the severe winter of 1952, much of Elko County was "snowed in." Local officials requested help from Fort Douglas in Utah for equipment to plow all the snow, but the commander at Fort Douglas refused. Austin made a phone call to his friend, Nevada senator Pat McCarran in Washington, D.C.; the equipment was soon on the way.

Austin, his wife and two children lived in a house on the main street in Wells. Part of the building was living quarters and part was telephone office. He joked that he always felt safe there because it was located between the police station and the Presbyterian church. He walked the streets of Wells, always finding his way with no problems.

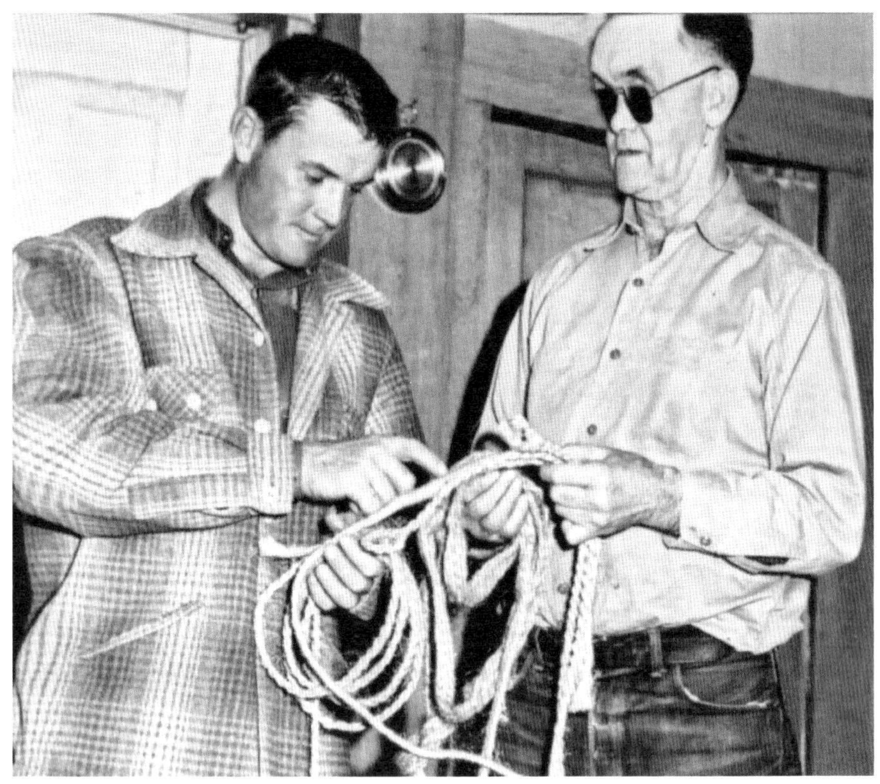

Austin Peltier (*right*) gives a braided bull rope to Gordon Wines (the author's late husband). *Courtesy of author's collection.*

One of his hobbies was braiding, with twine and rope, and he completed a wide variety of articles. He made hanging baskets from baling twine; nearly every woman in the county had one of his baskets full of plants. He braided ropes for bull riders to use at rodeos. A bull rope is very specialized, with several different designs and widths in the same rope and a handle braided into the rope. Peltier's bull ropes were well made and prized by those who owned them.

Austin was a remarkable man who dealt with the difficulties of life in a remarkable manner. He died in 1990 at the age of ninety.

II

Potts Hanging

The Rest of the Story

Everyone around Elko County knows about the Potts hanging in 1890. It's one of the best-known stories from this area's early history. The first and last execution of a woman in Nevada, it was also the first legal execution of a woman in the entire Pacific Coast region. Although Elizabeth and Josiah Potts insisted they were innocent to the very end, a jury, a judge and, ultimately, the state board of pardons all remained certain they were guilty of murder. The judge sentenced them to hang for their crime. The local sheriff was opposed to the death penalty, as were many county residents, but he did not prevail. Elizabeth and Josiah Potts died on a double gallows in the courtyard of the Elko County Courthouse on June 20, 1890, for the murder of Miles Faucett.

Elizabeth was a very large woman, weighing about two hundred pounds, and was obviously the boss in the Potts family. Josiah, a quiet, nervous little man, apparently did whatever Elizabeth told him to do. The evidence against them was quite damning, but they had an excuse for everything presented. Miles Faucett was a neighbor of Josiah and Elizabeth Potts in Carlin. He had lived with them earlier and then moved into his own place. He visited the Potts family on New Year's Day in 1888, and no one ever saw him again. When asked, the Pottses said he left for California to attend to business. Josiah and Elizabeth had his wagon, horse and many items from his house, but they claimed that Miles owed them money and had given these things in payment. The Pottses moved to Rock Springs, Wyoming, shortly after Miles's disappearance, and no one in Carlin thought any more about the whole affair.

Things soon started to unravel. A family moved into the old Potts house and reported strange noises, especially in the cellar under the house. (These noises were made by cats that could smell something there.) The family jokingly told people the place was haunted. However, when they heard the story about Miles Faucett disappearing during a visit to the house, it prompted the new tenants to take an iron rod and poke about in the dirt floor of the cellar. What they discovered was the grisly remains of a person, hacked to pieces and burned almost beyond recognition. Townspeople recognized a pocketknife found near the body as belonging to Miles. The finger of suspicion pointed to the Pottses.

The Elko County sheriff wired the authorities in Rock Springs and had them hold the Pottses on suspicion of murder. On the return trip to Elko, Josiah and Elizabeth told the sheriff that Miles had committed suicide at their house. Fearing that people would think they murdered him, they said they buried him in the cellar and left town.

The Elko County grand jury indicted them on a charge of murder. During their trial, Elizabeth said Miles had assaulted the Pottses' small daughter when he lived with them but that Elizabeth had not told Josiah for fear he would harm Miles. She also didn't tell the authorities, because she didn't want Josiah to know. Elizabeth testified that during his visit to their house on New Year's Day, Elizabeth told Josiah the story about their daughter. Josiah threatened to kill Miles, but they testified that Miles shot himself at that point rather than face his crime.

The jury didn't believe their stories, convicting them of first-degree murder. The judge sentenced them to death by hanging. The Elko County sheriff and 267 residents of the county signed a petition, which they then presented to the state board of pardons, asking for life imprisonment instead of the death sentence. The board denied the appeal.

The hanging was quite an infamous event. A double gallows was constructed in Placerville, California, and shipped in pieces to Elko. It was reassembled near the courthouse, and a high fence was built around the gallows to prevent the general public from watching. The press and law enforcement from around the state received printed invitations; fifty-two men attended. No women were invited or allowed at the event. Josiah died immediately, but the weights had not been adjusted properly for the much heavier Elizabeth. Her head was nearly severed. The bodies were taken to the Elko Cemetery and, after a few words by a local minister, were buried in the potter's field. Those watching the gruesome event crossed the street to the nearest saloon for a drink to help erase the memory of what had

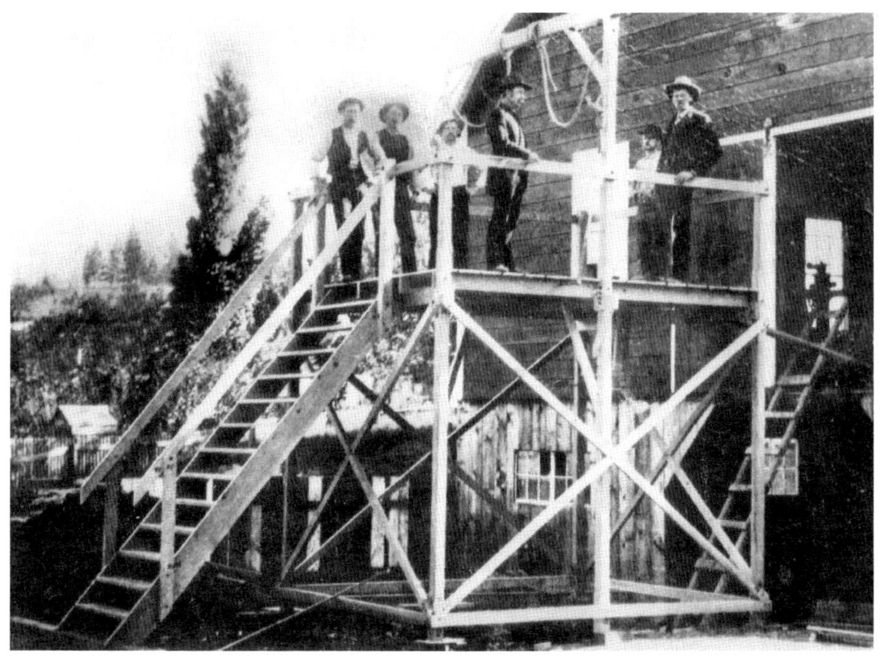

The double gallows, built in Placerville, California, and shipped to Elko. *Courtesy of Northeastern Nevada Museum.*

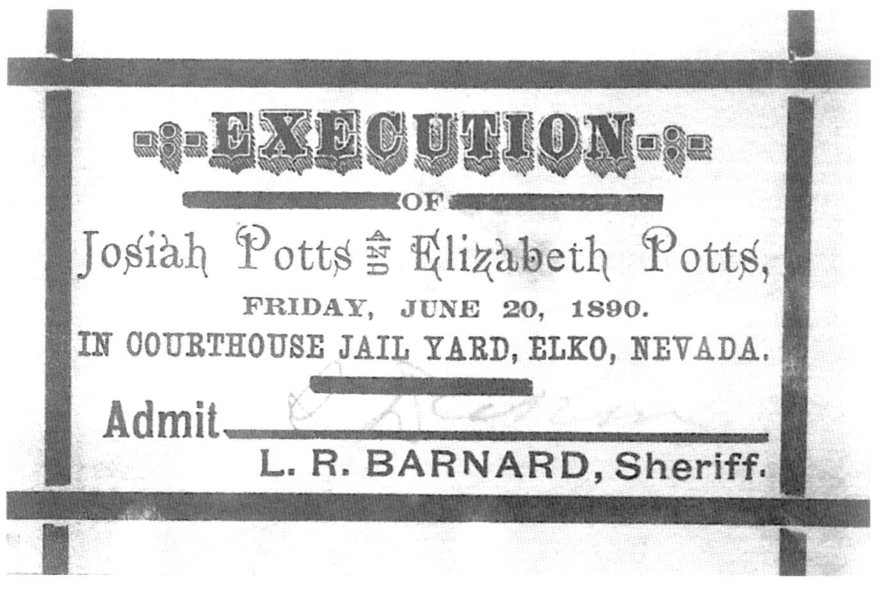

EXECUTION

OF

Josiah Potts and Elizabeth Potts,

FRIDAY, JUNE 20, 1890.

IN COURTHOUSE JAIL YARD, ELKO, NEVADA.

Admit ____________________

L. R. BARNARD, Sheriff.

The official invitation to the Pottses' hanging. *Courtesy of Northeastern Nevada Museum.*

happened. A gloom hung over Elko as men tried to defend what they had been called upon to do in the name of justice.

Evidence discovered later indicated that when Miles Faucett had known the Potts family in California years before, he was aware that Elizabeth was having an affair during that time with another man. Miles knew about the affair, but Josiah never found out. The Pottses later moved to Carlin, leaving her lover behind. Miles also moved to Carlin, where they remained friends, with only Elizabeth and Miles sharing her secret.

None of this came out during the trial, but no one knows what really transpired on the fateful night of the murder. To this day, some people think the Pottses were innocent. But considering all the evidence, most think they were guilty.

12

Hiram Chase

A Spirited Hero

Hiram Chase was a drunk. At least, he started out that way when he came to Elko in 1869, just as it was becoming a town. His job cutting wood for the new Central Pacific Railroad provided him with enough money for food, some clothes and a lot of whiskey. Trains in those days burned wood for power, and Hiram would spend his days cutting wood and his nights drinking hooch.

No one knew much about his life prior to his arrival in Elko. They only knew he was a native of the state of New York and had traveled to California on a ship in 1849, not to search for gold but to set up a merchandise store at the gold fields. Then, in 1869, he came to Elko as the new railroad came through. That's where this story begins.

He lived in a little cabin by the Humboldt River. One night, an apparition appeared to him as he sat drinking. The imagined visitor told him that his hands were the cause of all his problems. If he had no hands, he couldn't lift a bottle to his lips. This all seemed so real to Hiram that he dipped his hands in bacon grease, coated them with flour and thrust them into the stove. He continued doing this until the pain finally overtook him and he staggered to a nearby house, where he begged the people to shoot him to put him out of his misery. Instead, they called the local doctor, who finally had to amputate his arms just below the elbows.

After a long recovery, which he faced bravely, some friends helped Hiram obtain a small cart, from which he sold peanuts and candy on the streets of Elko. His happy and sincere demeanor won him many more friends, and his

"LIVE AND LET LIVE"

GROCERY STORE,

ELKO' - - NEVADA

H. CHASE, - PROPRIETOR.

Groceries, Provisions,

HARDWARE, GRAIN, ETC

In Quantities to Suit.

None but first-class' goods kept in stock. The leading and choicest brands of everything in the grocery line.

"Live and Let Live" is my motto.

Hiram Chase believed in advertising and regularly placed ads for his store in the local newspaper. *Courtesy of Northeastern Nevada Museum.*

business was quite successful. He was fitted with two hooks, which made his life somewhat easier. Although still disabled, he could do as much hard work in a day as the average full-bodied man.

Hiram eventually secured a small store and expanded his inventory. He loaded sacks of flour and sugar, cases of coal oil, boxes of canned goods and other heavy merchandise into his delivery wagon. He drove a spirited horse and handled the reins, wrapped around his hooks, as well as the best horseman in town. People would make their own change when they paid him. He continued to prosper and eventually moved up to a larger store. He sold nearly everything the citizens of the town and surrounding areas needed. Hiram lived in two rooms behind the store and never touched another drop of liquor.

Hiram became a beloved member of the community, and people admired his work ethic. He would carry people on his books until they had enough money to settle their accounts. Some would pay him at their next payday, and many ranchers would pay him once a year when they sold their livestock. He anonymously performed many acts of charity for the needy. Hiram was

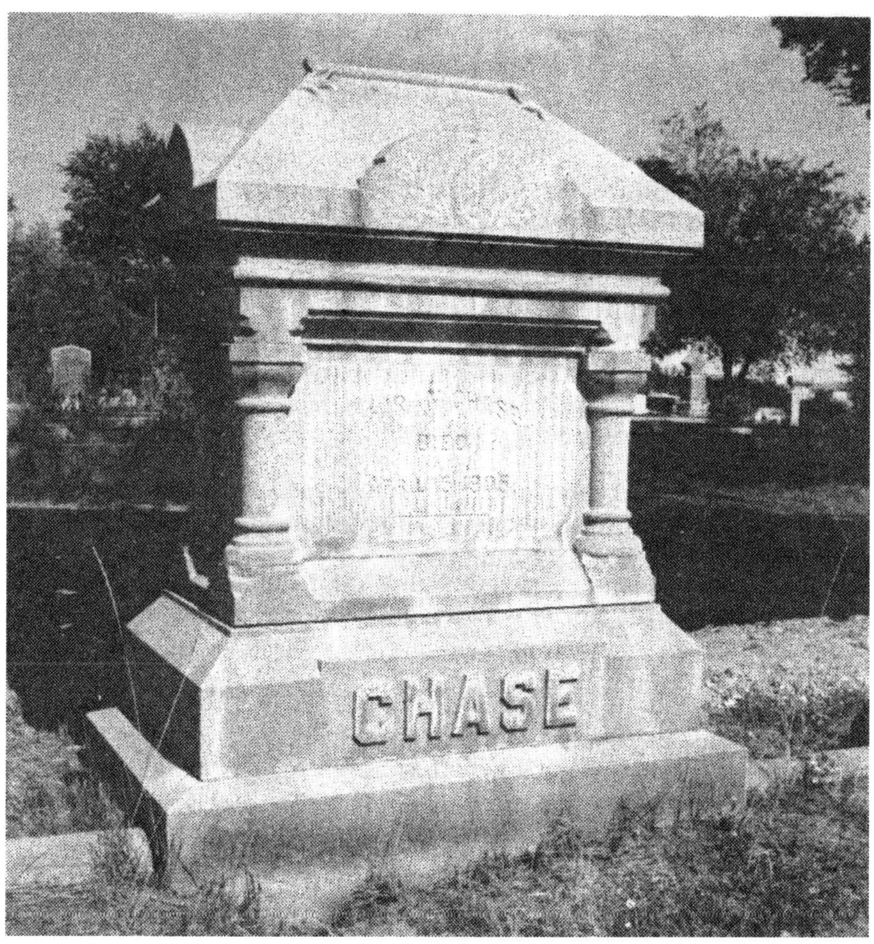

This gravestone marks the final resting place of Hiram Chase in the Elko Cemetery. *Courtesy of Northeastern Nevada Museum.*

a great friend to the children; those who went into his store always left with a gift of a piece of candy or chewing gum.

He continued this prosperous business for the next thirty-five years. Toward the end, he was ill for a few weeks and received the best medical attention available.

Hiram lived to be eighty-five years old and died on April 15, 1905. His funeral was a large affair. School was dismissed for the day, allowing all of the children, his special friends, to attend the funeral. The local newspaper reported that the funeral and the cortege to the cemetery were among the largest ever seen in Elko. He had driven his horse and wagon at the rear of every funeral procession in town, but for his funeral, a friend drove it, loaded with flowers, right behind the hearse.

A search to locate any living relatives turned up empty, and his nearly $50,000 estate eventually went to the State of Nevada.

When he arrived in Elko, he was a ne'er-do-well and a drunk. But thirty-six years later, he received a hero's sendoff to the candy store in the sky.

13

Maude Bolton

A Rocky Start to a Smooth Marriage

Maude Bolton was a typical ranch wife in Elko County in the early 1900s, happily married to Ham Bolton for fifty-eight years. They were a popular couple in Elko County, with many friends, who all believed them to be an ideal couple—and they were. The few who knew how the marriage started out would never have guessed that it would turn out that way. The first couple of months were very rocky. Here's how it began.

Hansford B. "Ham" Bolton was born in Virginia in 1883. When he was twenty years old, he decided to go west. He had a cousin, J.J. Hylton, who owned several ranches and a mercantile in Skelton, Mound Valley, in Elko County. He had sent glowing reports back to Virginia about the vast ranching country of northeastern Nevada.

When Ham traveled to Nevada, he went through Texas. He apparently had friends there and tarried a while. He was quite smitten with the young daughter of his friends, but she was only thirteen, a bit too young to sweep her off her feet and take her to Nevada with him, so he went on alone. He worked on his cousin's ranch for several years, but the yellow rose in Texas was always on his mind.

She was Maude McGinley, and she thought of him often, too. However, she didn't think she would ever see him again. Born in Texas in 1889, she had never been too far from home.

In 1904, after two years in Nevada, Ham traveled back to Texas. He was twenty-two by then, and Maude was fifteen.

He courted her for a time, and they decided to marry. They weren't sure how people would react, and they didn't have much money for a nice party and dinner after a marriage, which was customary. So they decided to elope. Ham came calling one afternoon. Maude was dressed in her best frock and hat, but no one suspected anything, because girls always dressed nicely when beaus were coming to call.

They went by horse and buggy to the county seat, where they obtained a marriage license. They asked where they could find a minister and discovered that the only one in the area was a cotton farmer who lived out of town and wouldn't be around until Sunday.

Ham and Maude got directions to the minister's farm and set off for another long ride. When they arrived, Ham went to the house to seek the minister, and Maude stayed in the buggy. She was feeling a little apprehensive by then and secretly hoped the minister's wife would invite them to be married in her parlor. But Ham came out of the house, waved to her and started off on foot through the farmland. She felt the first feelings of panic; had he changed his mind and was leaving the country, with her sitting in the buggy? Her fears were short-lived, and Ham shortly returned with a man dressed in work clothes. He was the minister, and he did not invite them into his home. He performed the wedding by the side of the road.

Ham wanted to return to Nevada. He was sure he could get another job there and they could make a good start to their new life. Ham left immediately for Nevada, and Maude was to follow in three weeks.

The train ride to Elko was a frightening and lonely experience for her, and the unfamiliar desert scenery didn't make her feel any better. She hoped her new home would look better than this.

As the train approached Elko, she checked her dress and hat to make sure she looked pretty for her new husband as she got off the train. She hadn't seen Ham for three weeks, and she fully expected him to rush up and give her a big kiss—but he wasn't there. She went into the depot and waited. He was probably just a few minutes late, she thought; he would surely be there before long. She kept making excuses for him in her mind. Every few minutes she would get up and go to the window, hoping to see him ride up. She waited all afternoon—no Ham. She began to feel a panic rising in her throat. Here she was, a thousand miles from home, a tender fifteen years old and quite sure by now that her new husband had abandoned her and she would never see him again. It was hard to hold back the tears.

As evening set in, the stationmaster advised her to go across the street and get a room at the Commercial Hotel, which she did. She didn't sleep well that night.

Morning came, and still no husband. She was positive by now that he had abandoned her. Then she remembered that Ham's brother worked at the Hylton and Hanna store at Skelton, in Mound Valley, so she decided to call him before she gave up completely. She found the nearest phone and called her brother-in-law. He told her that Ham was cooking on the chuck wagon for a crew gathering wild horses and wouldn't be back for a week or so. Ham had left word that if a girl named Maude arrived and called, he should tell her to catch the mail stage to Skelton. Apparently Ham wasn't completely sure she would show up.

The trip to Skelton took all day. By then, the scared, unhappy fifteen-year-old was convinced she had made the worst mistake of her young life.

A local woman, Mrs. Woods, saw her get off the stage, knew who she must be and took her home with her. That cheered Maude a little bit. She stayed with Mrs. Woods and, except for the absence of her husband, began to feel a little better. Then she contracted scarlet fever. She was very sick, but the kind Mrs. Woods nursed her back to health. After all this, still no husband.

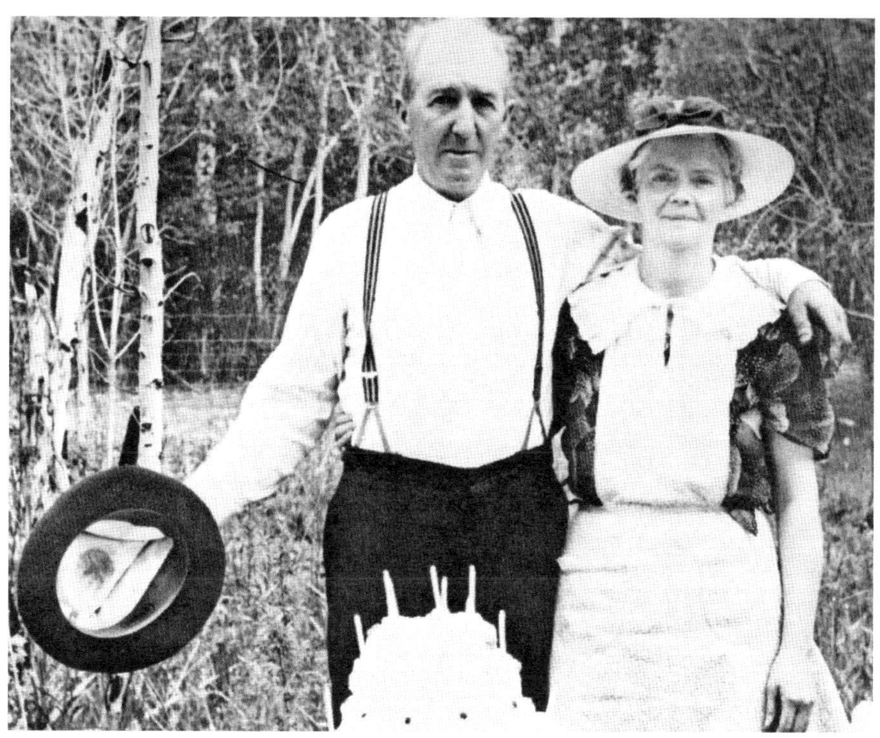

Maude and Ham Bolton at a picnic celebrating their fiftieth wedding anniversary. *Courtesy of Northeastern Nevada Museum.*

Finally, several weeks later, Ham showed up. Maude slowly realized she had made the right choice after all.

The happy couple spent the next fifty-eight years on ranches, side by side to the end. In spite of its rocky beginning, the marriage not only lasted but thrived. She died in 1962, at age seventy-three, and he died in 1968, at age eighty-five.

14

Elko Airport

Those Magnificent Men (and Women) in Their Flying Machines

The first air flight in the United States, by the Wright brothers, happened in 1903. Just sixteen years later, Elko had an airport, and interesting things started happening.

Elko mayor A.J. McBride received a telegram from the U.S. Post Office Department in March 1919. It wanted a runway in Elko on which planes could land. There were only a few specifications: the area should be six hundred feet by twelve hundred feet and hard enough to drive a motorcycle on. There needed to be a cross, made of cloth, twenty feet long on the ground to mark the spot from the sky. In one corner, there should be a stick with a five-foot cloth tied to it to show the direction of the wind. The people in Elko were excited about this project and immediately went to work. In short order, they had an airport. The site was approximately where the current airport is located.

Airmail flights began on the East Coast as early as 1918, and by 1919, plans were underway for the Woodrow Wilson Aerial Highway. It would go from New York to Cleveland, Ohio; Chicago; Iowa City, Iowa; Omaha and North Platte, Nebraska; Cheyenne and Rock Springs, Wyoming; Salt Lake City, Utah; Elko and Reno, Nevada; and San Francisco, California.

The airport at Elko needed to pass inspection to make sure it was satisfactory. A survey crew, including the famous flying ace Eddie Rickenbacker, flew into Elko in August 1920. They determined that the little landing strip was just fine, but the excited citizens of Elko decided to make it

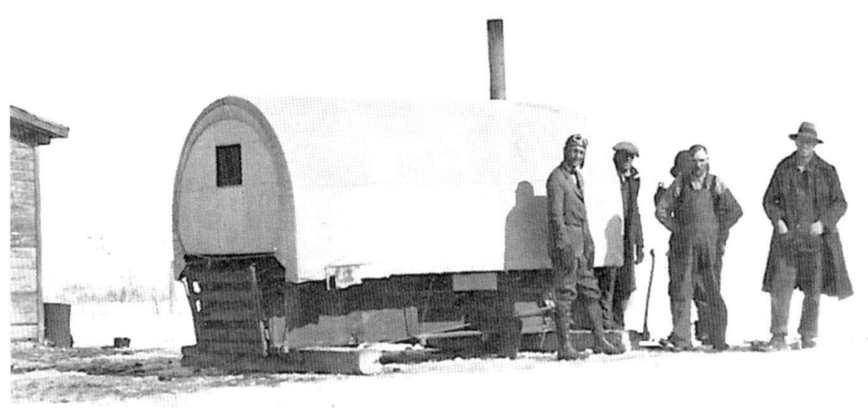

A sheep camp served as the first pilot's office at the new Elko Airport. *Courtesy of Northeastern Nevada Museum.*

even better and enlarged it to a four-way landing strip. They put up tents to serve as hangars and used an old sheep camp wagon for an office. The Post Office Department said it was the best airport west of Cheyenne. The tent buildings at the airport didn't hold up well. Wind destroyed one of them, and the other burned to the ground. They were gradually replaced with real buildings.

The first flight through Elko was on September 9, 1919. The plane landed successfully, but things didn't go so well after that. Crashes became common occurrences. Some were fatal, but most were just mechanical failures and the pilots survived; as fliers were usually good mechanics, they could fix the problems themselves. It was before the days of radios in planes, so if the pilot needed parts, he would hike from the crash site to the nearest telephone. Pilots usually carried a rifle in the plane—not to protect the mail but to shoot something to eat if they crashed away from civilization.

Gradually, airmail service secured better aircraft, but there were still many accidents. Pilot Paul Scott went down three times in snowstorms in the winter of 1922. He either crashed or landed out in the sagebrush eleven different times during his mail-flying career.

In 1922, airmail pilot Kenneth Unger crash-landed near Secret Pass in the Ruby Mountains and filed the following accident report:

> *I was crossing the Rubbie* [*sic*] *Mountains at 10,500 feet when I broke a set of gears and landed in a very small field in the Secret Pass. A rancher riding range saw me land and rode over and let me take his horse to ride to the nearest ranch. After phoning to Elko for help, I started back to the ship on the horse. I started to mount and the horse took off in a climbing turn before I got in the seat and had my safety belt fastened. To make a long story short, I over-controlled her nose, went down and spun or side-slipped, I don't know which, into the ground at great speed. I broke my left ankle and was well shaken up in my second landing. After filling the air with smoke for a few minutes, I got the beat again and we took off on a gentle lope and returned to the ship. Help came. We repaired the motor and I flew the ship to Elko. There I had the ankle set by the best doctor in town. I had to borrow a pair of crutches…and had the boys at the field tack a strip to the rudder bar so I could pull as well as push. This made up for the loss of my left foot. I took off for Salt Lake City with the regular mail as usual. Motto: Always be sure you have your safety belt on before you take off on a western horse.*

In 1923, the American Legion sponsored a flying circus. George Babcock stood on the wing of a plane, then hung by his knees from the landing gear and finally parachuted into the rodeo grounds to the cheers of the local citizens.

A historic event took place in 1926: the first commercial airmail flight after passage of the Kelly Act. In 1925, Congress passed HR 7064, "An Act to encourage commercial aviation and to authorize the Postmaster General to contract for Air Mail Service." This law directed the U.S. Post Office Department to contract with private airlines to carry the mail over designated routes. The 1926 flight, from Pasco, Washington, to Elko, was the first feeder airline to connect from the hinterlands into the main line, the Woodrow Wilson Aerial Highway. Walter Varney bid on the route from Pasco, Washington, to Elko, through Boise, and received the contract. The first nationwide flight was on April 6, 1926, with Leon Cuddleback as pilot. They loaded 207 pounds of mail on a small Laird Swallow biplane, and Cuddleback flew to Boise, stopped and picked up more mail and flew on to Elko. At ninety miles an hour, it took him nine hours. Nearly the entire population of Elko turned out to see him land. The return flight was not so successful. Pilot Franklin Rose was downed in the middle of the vast Owyhee

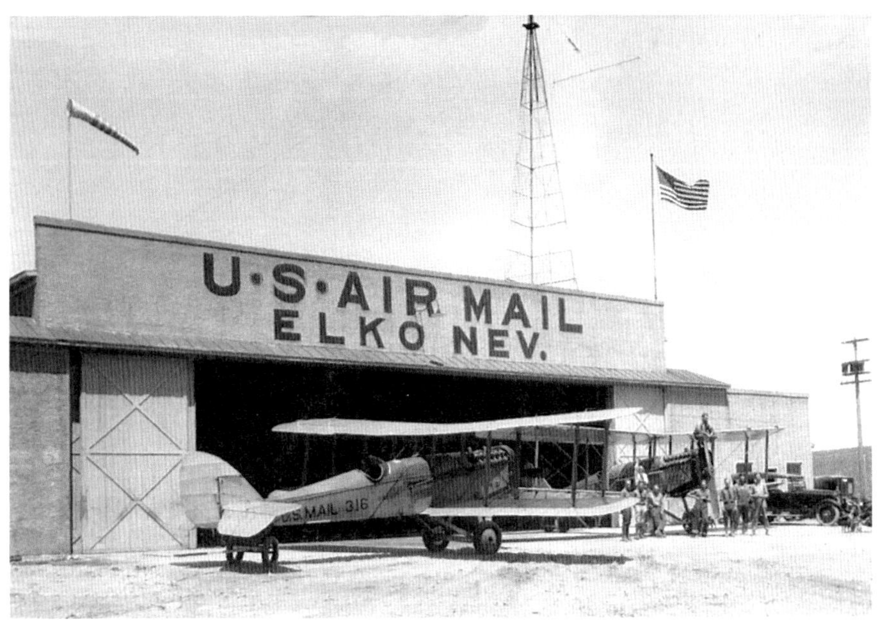

Several pilots stand near one of the airplanes used in the new commercial airmail flights into the Elko Airport. *Courtesy of Northeastern Nevada Museum.*

Desert by a storm and was immediately tied up by two moonshiners, who thought the "U.S." on the side of the airplane meant it was manned by a federal prohibition agent searching for whiskey stills. Rose finally convinced them who he was, they untied him and he hiked for two days, carrying 98 pounds of mail, to the nearest phone. That flight took three days. There were two more wrecks in the period of the first week. This mail route continued for three years but finally moved to Salt Lake City because of better weather—inclement weather was determined to be the cause of most of the crashes.

In January 1929, Frank Barber and two passengers left Elko, headed to Salt Lake City with the mail. Barber was an experienced pilot but had never flown this route. He encountered a blizzard and crashed into the Ruby Mountains. The three men were injured but survived. When the plane didn't arrive in Salt Lake City, another plane flew out to search for them. The pilot saw them, tipped his wings to indicate he knew where they were and flew on to Elko. A search party consisting of local ranchers and a U.S. Forest Service employee headed for the wreck, but the snow became too deep for their horses and they had to continue on foot. The pilot from Salt Lake continued to circle, dropping flares to guide them to the wreck. The rescuers reached the downed plane and struggled to get the men off the mountain. They took them by sleigh to the nearest railroad and on to Salt Lake City for medical attention. Another group of ranchers went up a few days later and retrieved the six hundred pounds of mail on the plane. The airline company retrieved the engine and instrument panel the next summer; as far as anyone knows, the body of the plane is still up there in the mountains.

A number of famous pilots landed in Elko through the early years, some on purpose and some not. On June 5, 1931, six years before her final flight, Amelia Earhart landed at the Elko Airport to refuel. Other notables who

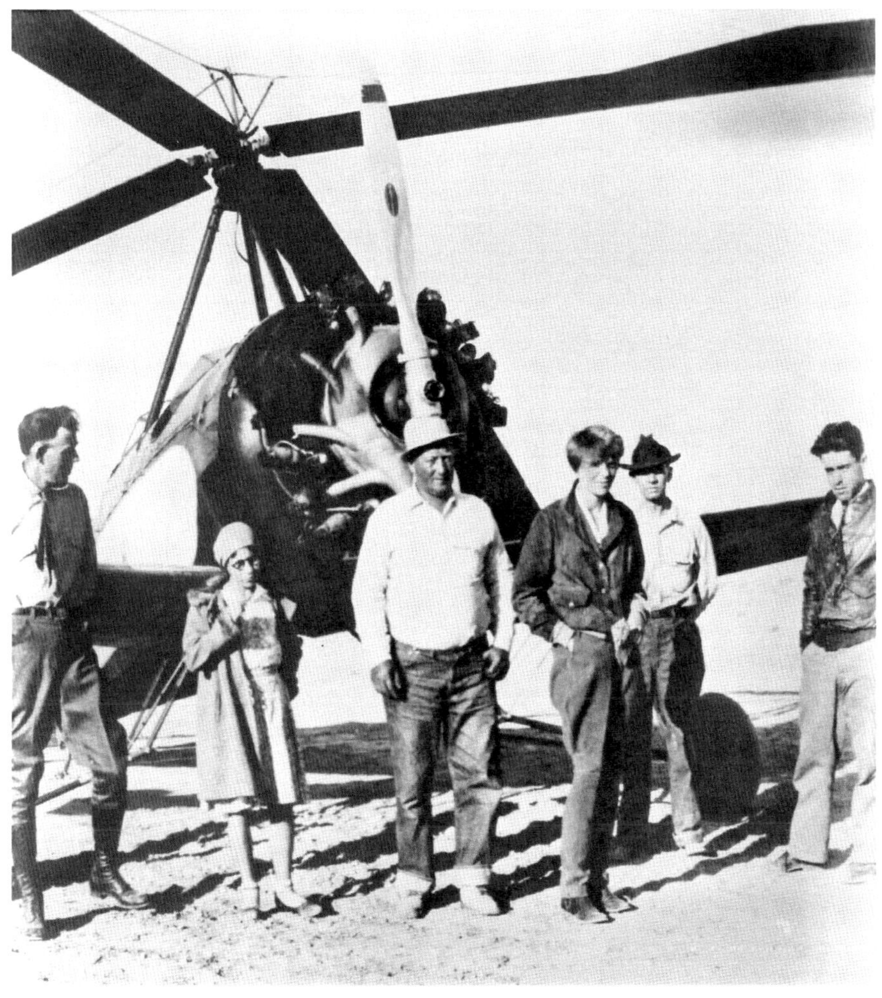

Amelia Earhart (*third from right*) stopped in Elko to refuel on a cross-country flight several years before her fatal last flight. *Courtesy of Northeastern Nevada Museum.*

flew into Elko included Richard E. Byrd in 1926, in the plane in which he reportedly flew over the North Pole. In 1928, Charles Lindbergh radioed that he was low on fuel and would be landing at the airport. By the time he arrived, half the town was there to greet him. Wiley Post, the pilot who later died in a crash with Will Rogers, landed in Elko several years before that fateful flight.

With many improvements and upgrades through the years, the Elko Airport continues to serve as the only commercial airport in Elko County.

15

JOHANNA LOFDAHL

Denmark in the Sagebrush

If there was ever an optimistic, glass-half-full kind of person, it was Johanna Lofdahl. Life was not always kind, especially in her later years, but she never complained. She looked back and said it was all good; she was glad it turned out the way it did.

She was born in Sweden in 1856. In 1880, she married August Lofdahl, when they were both twenty-four. Soon after, the couple moved to Copenhagen, Denmark. August and Johanna had six children. The youngest, Hans Christian, was born when Johanna was forty-five years old and was developmentally challenged.

August was a farmer, and the Lofdahls developed a highly successful, beautiful farm in Denmark. They were very happy there, but the children kept hearing of great opportunities in America and wanted to emigrate. Their oldest son, Carl, was the first to do so. In 1904, in his early twenties, he sailed from Copenhagen to Ellis Island in New York and on west by train. He secured a job working for the Western Pacific Railroad as boss of the crew that was constructing a telegraph line next to the company's railroad through Nevada. In 1907, his work took him to Tobar and Clover Valley in Elko County. He was attracted to the ads for farmland available in the area. Although there was nothing but sagebrush flats as far as the eye could see, Carl was intrigued with the idea that the area could be productive farmland. He envisioned a place similar to his family's farm in Denmark.

While he was working near Tobar, his sister Hedvig traveled to America, also coming through Ellis Island. She was only eighteen and traveled alone.

She became the cook for Carl's crew and soon changed her name to Helen. In 1909, she married Joseph "J.B." McDaniel, who worked for her brother. She spoke no English, and he spoke only English, but they seemed to manage just fine.

Emma, another daughter of August and Johanna, was the next to come to America. She also came alone, but by a different route, from England to Canada and then to the United States. Oscar, age eighteen, came next, also through Canada.

By 1909, only August, Johanna and their two youngest children, Einer, thirteen, and Hans Christian, eight, were left in Denmark. At age fifty-three, they sold their beautiful farm and sailed for America.

Then the trouble began. The immigration officers in Quebec deemed Hans Christian mentally unfit because he could not answer their questions; they refused to allow him to enter the country. They couldn't return to Denmark, because they had sold everything and most of their family was already in Nevada. They made the hard decision for August and Einer to continue on to Nevada; Johanna and Hans Christian boarded another ship and returned to Copenhagen. Johanna was determined to try another port of entry into America, with what she hoped would be better results. Upon their arrival in Denmark, she and her small son boarded a ship headed for New York; this time it worked. She accomplished all this while speaking very little English.

After a difficult train trip across the country, Johanna and Han Christian finally arrived in Wells and were reunited with the rest of the family. The migration of the entire group took six years.

Carl had taken up a homestead, in addition to his railroad work, near Tobar. The land developers had constructed a small hotel, several stores and an office where they sold people on the idea of farming in the desert. Advertisements featuring large apples, supposedly grown on trees in the area, enticed many to move to the sagebrush flat and attempt farming. The name, Tobar, came from one of the first settlers, who owned a bar. He put up a sign with an arrow pointing to his establishment that read "To Bar." The name is pronounced "Tow-bar," and the town is currently only a few foundations in the sagebrush.

J.B. and Helen had also taken up homesteads on Tobar Flat, where they were trying to establish a new farm. When Johanna arrived, she was taken aback by the bleak landscape that greeted her but was pleasantly surprised to learn her first grandchild would be born shortly. The new arrival was named Helen Johanna, after her mother and grandmother.

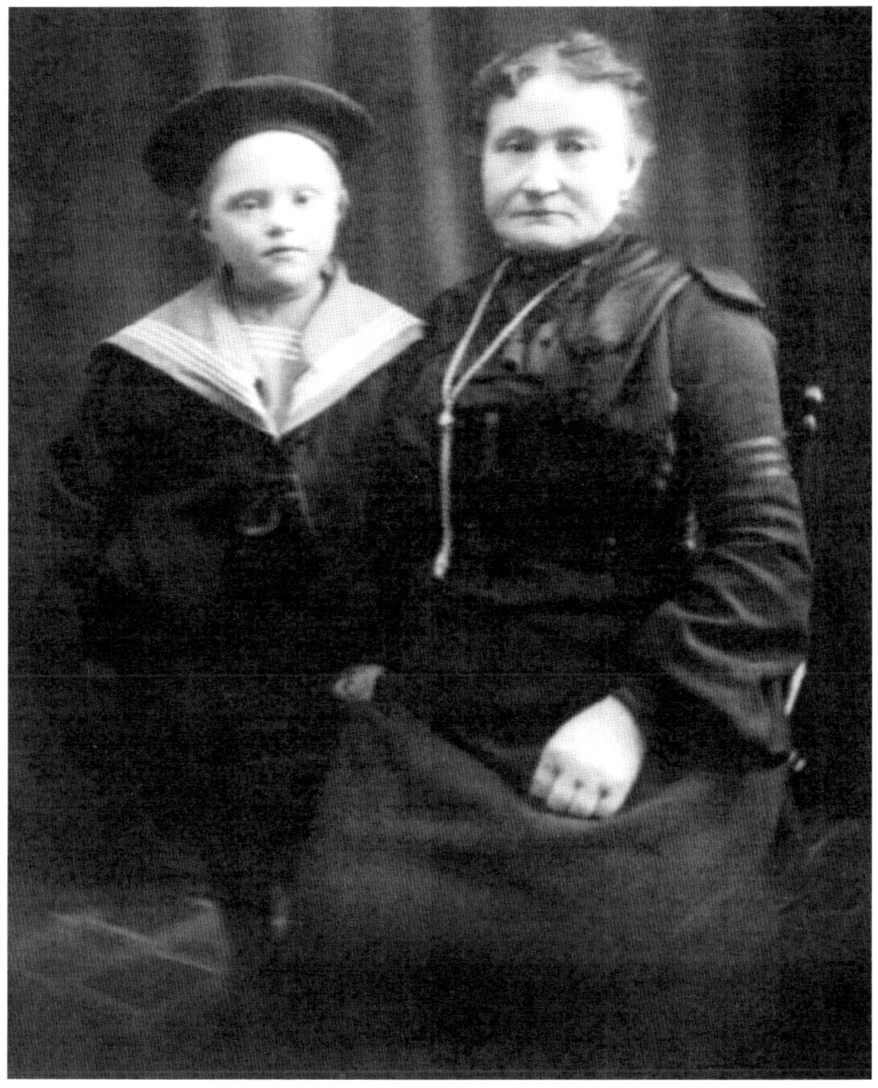

Johanna Lofdahl and her youngest son, Hans Christian, are seen as they left Denmark to travel to America the second time. *Courtesy of Milton Sharp.*

August and Johanna acquired a homestead nearby, but life was not easy for them. The land developers touted it as a farming paradise, but it was not. There was very little water available, and in many years, crickets and rabbits destroyed their crops. Tobar Flat was unlike nearby Clover Valley, nestled at the foot of the Ruby Mountains, where there was plenty of water and prosperous ranches.

Most of the family and other homesteaders moved on to greener pastures. Finally, only August and Johanna and daughter Helen and her husband, J.B., were left in the area. They called it Little Denmark, although it never resembled the beautiful farm they left behind. August, a very good farmer, managed to build up a respectable place, but he was getting older and it became harder. J.B. always worked away from home, at nearby mines and ranches, in order to earn money. Helen and their children would stay home and try to farm.

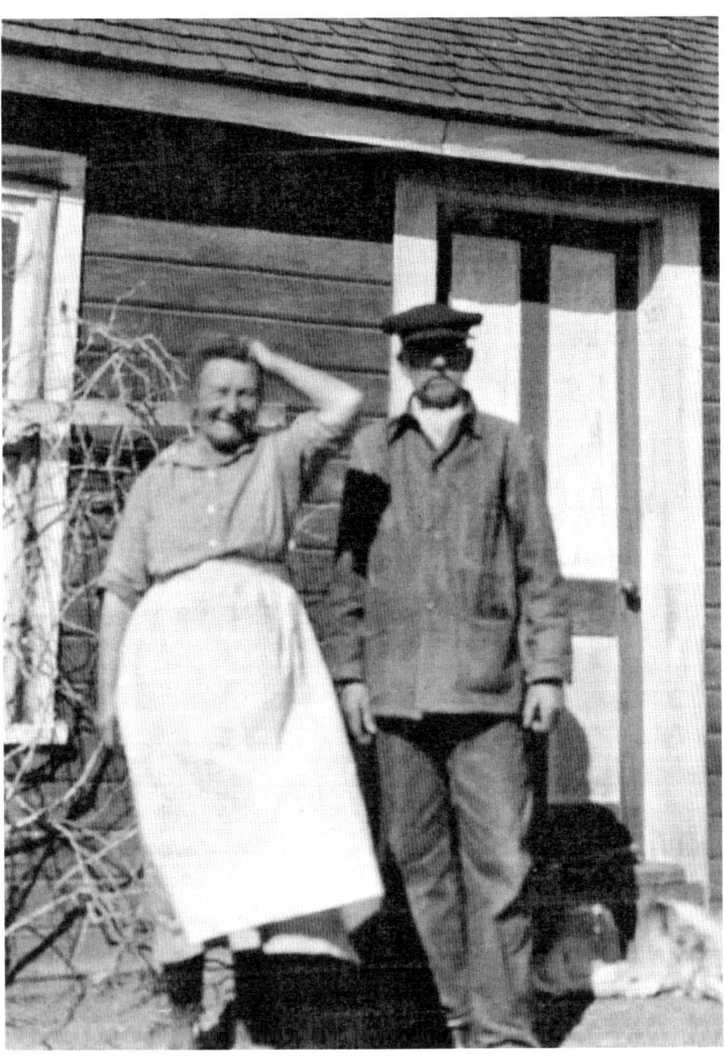

Johanna Lofdahl with her husband, August, in front of their home on Tobar Flat. *Courtesy of Milton Sharp.*

In her later years, Johanna told her story to her granddaughter Helen Johanna, who preserved it for future generations. Johanna recalled how they wanted a farm similar to the one they left in Denmark, where they had pigs, chickens, ducks, cows and at least one horse. Ducks were out of the question because of the lack of water, but they had everything else—except a pig. They determined to get a pig, so they made a trip in their wagon to a neighbor in Clover Valley, who sold them one. They tied the pig up, loaded it on the wagon and headed home. It kept up a continuous squealing and kicking, finally kicking loose and jumping out of the wagon. Johanna recalled that the Lofdahls still wore wooden shoes, much to the amusement of their neighbors. As Johanna told the story, she said, "Now, wooden shoes worn by the cleverest and lightest of foot make a good deal of noise, and Bedstefar [the Danish word for "grandfather," a name she always called August] was neither light-footed nor clever; your imagination will tell you how the pig felt when he heard such a noise." As August ran after the pig, the wooden shoes made such a clatter that it scared the pig, who ran even faster. Johanna recalled, "I stayed in the wagon and laughed until Bedstefar became angry. When the pig got tired, he took to standing behind a bush, listening tensely, while Bedstefar crept up, almost near enough to catch him by the leg. When he made a grab for him, the pig would give a scared 'woof' and they would be off again." August finally did catch the pig and sat down and held it by the leg while they both rested. He then tied the pig up again and put it in the wagon, and they finally got it home.

Johanna also told about harvesting hay that they managed to raise in a small meadow on their little farm. All the neighbors in Clover Valley had horse-drawn haying equipment, which they offered to loan to the Lofdahls, but she said, "No thanks. [We know] how to do it without such nonsense." They preferred to do it the way they did in Denmark. They hooked a sledge behind their horse and grabbed a handful of grass, sawed it off with a kitchen knife, picked the foxtail and cheat grass out of it and lay it on the sledge. Little by little, the haystack grew, and when they had a full load, they took it to the barn, where they would unload it by hand. This went on for several days, until the horse, Old Nellie, tired of all the waiting and walked away with nearly a full load of hay. August started out in his wooden shoes to stop the horse, but the noise startled her. Taking off at a run, the horse soon overturned the sledge and dumped the entire load. Johanna, telling the story, said, "Back in the meadow, Bedstefar made blue smoke rise in the placid air as the Danish language was made full use of in telling his opinion of horses in general." They finally borrowed modern haying equipment from the neighbors.

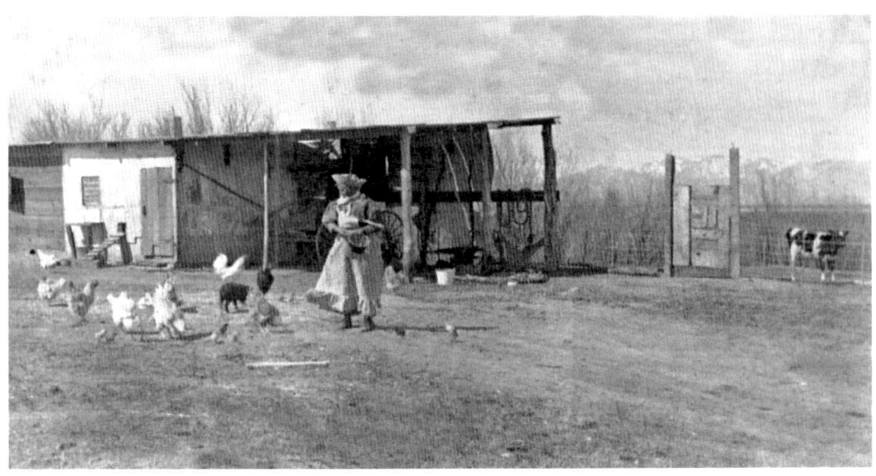

Johanna Lofdahl feeding the chickens at their farm. *Courtesy of Milton Sharp.*

Hans Christian died when he was fourteen; in 1926, at age seventy, August also died. By then, the McDaniels had given up and moved to Wells, where J.B. became a successful businessman. He built a motel, two gas stations and a hotel. With access to better automobiles and roads, people were traveling more and needed gas and a place to spend the night as they traveled through Wells.

Johanna refused to leave her little home in the desert, staying there alone for the next ten years. She finally, reluctantly, moved to Wells but was still fiercely independent and refused to live with the McDaniels. She stayed in a small house behind their home.

As she told the story of her life to her granddaughter, she talked about visiting the old place a few years later. "Little Denmark still exists but in what a sad state!" she said.

> *The once beautiful meadow is burned and sagebrush is springing up everywhere. Patches of glaring white alkali are staring from along the edges of what was once the meadow. The willows are practically dead. The cozy mud barn and chicken-coop have been kicked down by wild horses, fighting for shelter in the winter. The well, in which had once hung two wooden buckets balanced on a pulley, is caved in and dilapidated....The house is a sorry sight for anyone who had once lived in it and loved it. The windows have been knocked out, the tarpaper ripped off by the wind, the door half off its hinges hanging diagonally across the doorway. The lofts and the bunks, which were used for beds, are full of the nests of pack-rats. The place in which had grown a beautiful yellow rosebush boasts a great*

> *greasewood brush which nods spitefully in the breeze. Ah! It is better not to go to see it….The memories are many and dear! The sight hurts more than can be imagined. Some day it is better the wind take the remains and scatter them, hide them in the sagebrush. Then the temptation to go and see how things are will be gone.*

In 1949, J.B. was elected mayor of Wells. The entire community mourned when he was tragically killed in a car wreck during his first term. Children of Helen and J.B. became prominent business owners in the area. Their youngest son, Joseph McDaniel, became an attorney and served for many years as district attorney and then district court judge in Elko.

Johanna died in 1945 at age eighty-nine. Toward the end of her life, as she related her story to her granddaughter, Johanna had only good things to say about the difficulties in her life; she never regretted leaving Demark and coming to America.

16
Tez

Better on a Horse than a Car

During the Mexican Revolution, General Pancho Villa forced many people into his army, including the Yaqui Indians. Albino Tais, known as Tez, and his family were among these. Villa would either brand or earmark those in his army, so he could identify them if they deserted. Tez was branded on the shoulder. Those who did desert the army were usually captured and tortured before Villa killed them. Most of Tez's family was eventually killed, but he managed to escape. He was shot in the ankle, and the scar from that wound would bother him for the rest of his life. Tez could not read or write, because education was not a high priority during his difficult early years.

Tez finally made his way to California, out of the reach of Pancho Villa. He spent the next few years working on ranches in California, southeastern Oregon and finally into Nevada. He went to work for the 25 Ranch near Battle Mountain, Nevada, and spent the rest of his life there, working for several different owners.

In those days, there were no fences between most of the large ranches in northern Nevada, so cattle would often end up with those from neighboring places. Each ranch would send a "rep" to an adjoining ranch to help with branding in the spring and gathering the cattle in the fall. The rep would take the cattle to the home ranch for the winter.

Tez was always the rep for the 25 Ranch at Squaw Valley Ranch, owned by Ellison Ranching Company, in northwestern Elko County. Each of these ranches ran thousands of head of cattle, and by the time the animals were

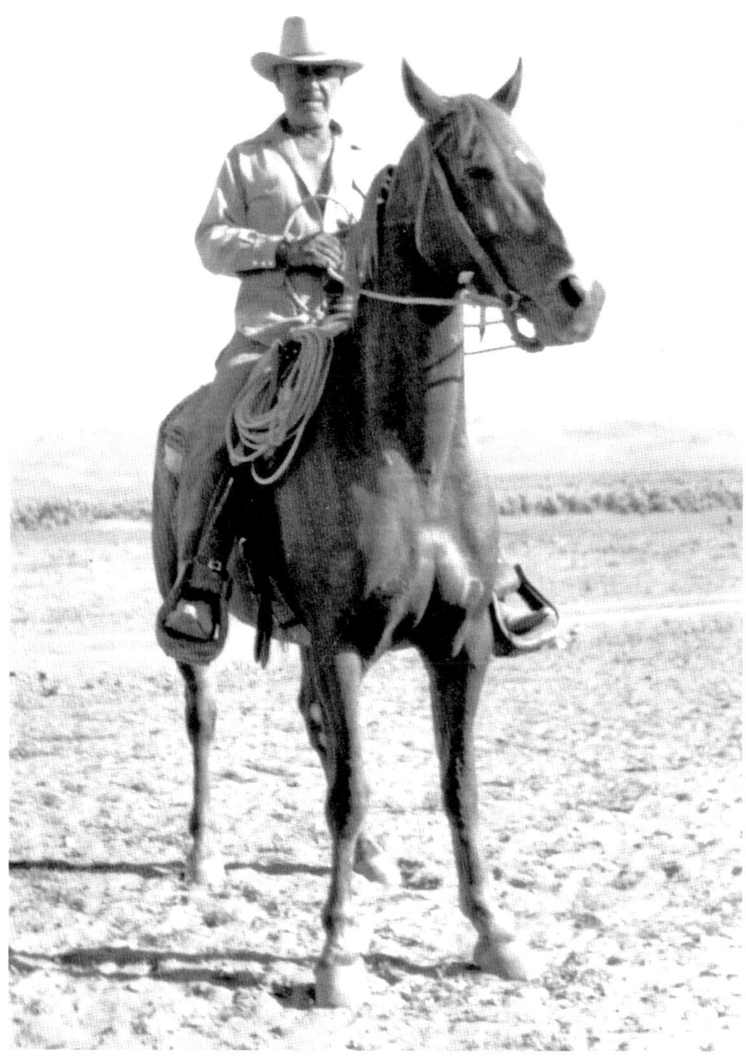

Albino "Tez" Tais at Squaw Valley Ranch, gathering cattle that belonged to the 25 Ranch near Battle Mountain. *Courtesy of Les Sweeney.*

gathered in the fall, the 25 would have several hundred head that had been sorted out of the Ellison cattle. Tez would drive them back to the home ranch, a three-day trip.

He was an accomplished horseman, and the horses in his string were top-notch. He was an excellent roper, but typical of many ropers, both then and now, he was missing a thumb. When a cowboy ropes an animal, he secures the rope around the saddle horn, and fingers and thumbs sometimes get caught in the dallies.

Tez had a happy, fun-loving personality. Cowboys who knew him could tell many amusing stories. Les Sweeney grew up on the Squaw Valley Ranch, where his father was the general manager. Les recalls many of these stories. He said when Tez was on horseback, he was the best, but he was a disaster when driving an automobile.

Tez started driving at a young age, and he never improved. When he was still working in California, he took a company pickup to town and went around a curve too fast; it rolled and ended up on its top. He walked home. When asked where the truck was, he replied, in his broken English, "He fall down, all his feet up."

Les continued with the stories. Tez bought a car for himself while working in northern Nevada: a Chrysler touring car. One day, he missed a curve on the road and drove into a ditch. The car turned over and landed on top of him. He lay under the car for quite a while before someone came along to help him. It was a long time before he got another car, but he finally did.

One day he announced, "I buy new machine." He always referred to cars as machines. It was a Ford, but he called it a Chryslerford.

Tez had trouble figuring out the gearshift in cars, and everyone around would move away when he started out, as they were not sure if he would put it in reverse or in a forward gear. He usually had the best chance of getting it started in second gear. It would stay there, no matter where he was going. Occasionally he started in first gear, and it would stay there the whole trip. He never drove very fast, but he would never slow down in time, either. He always had to slam on the brakes when he needed to stop. When he drove to one of the ranches where he worked, he usually didn't stop in time for the gates and would drive right through them. He had a dog he called George that started out riding with Tez in the front seat. After being slammed into the dashboard too many times, George started riding in the back.

Tez was driving in Battle Mountain one day where Main Street ran parallel to the railroad tracks through town. Raymond Orbide, a local rancher, pulled up to the railroad crossing in his truck and stopped to let a train pass. Tez turned the corner and ran into the back of Orbide's truck. George hit the dash, and the truck lurched ahead about three feet, almost hitting the train. When the sheriff showed up, he asked Tez why he ran into the truck, and he said, "Orbide he stop in the meedle of the road like a dead cow, no lights or nothin." The wreck totaled his Chryslerford.

He bought another Cryslerford but soon ran over a large boulder and destroyed that car, also.

All of the cars were used when he bought them, but he finally purchased a brand-new pickup. Sometime later, on a good stretch of road, straight with no gates, he rolled the pickup. No one was ever sure why—he wasn't, either.

Later, someone noticed that George wasn't with him anymore. When asked where the dog was, Tez said, "Last time I teepit over peekup, George he git-a-scare, he never did come back."

In all of his accidents, he was never hurt. He always thought they were funny. He died in 1960, at about seventy years of age. He was on horseback, not in an automobile, and he still had the brand on his shoulder.

Tez was a favorite with all the buckaroos he worked with and with everyone who knew him. Pancho Villa lost a good man.

17

Bob White

Was He Really Guilty?

Robert H. White of Elko was executed in the Nevada State Penitentiary on June 2, 1930, for the first-degree murder of Louis Lavell. The evidence at his trial was purely circumstantial but compelling enough that the jury convicted. Was he really guilty?

There were two sides to Bob White, and many people didn't really know him. There were many reasons, before the murder, for some people to think he was not capable of such a thing. He had a number of different jobs; one of them was driving a school bus, where he was a favorite of the kids.

When anyone would get sick at school, he was always willing to show up with his bus and take them home. He also owned and operated a restaurant and had a taxi service. He was a big, jovial man—six feet tall, 280 pounds—and most people in Elko liked him.

Bob White had another side that many people didn't know. He was involved in illegal gambling and bootlegging activities in Elko. Gambling was not yet legal in Nevada, and Prohibition was in force in the entire country.

In the days before the murder, Bob had another problem. His wife, Kathryne, wanted to travel to Ireland and kept harassing him about it. At the moment, he was short of money and couldn't afford to buy her the tickets she needed, which made his life rather unpleasant.

Bob White had two close friends: Louis Lavell, known as Louie the Greek, and Mike Connis. The three of them worked together running crooked card games at local hotels. That was a good source of income for Bob, as was his restaurant and his bus driving, but he always seemed to be a little short of money.

Louie the Greek had recently come into some money. Bob and Mike knew he had over $1,000 in cash in his pockets and some expensive jewelry. On Sunday, May 6, 1928, Mike saw Louie and Bob get into Bob's car about 11:00 p.m. That was the last time anyone saw Louie the Greek alive.

Two local couples had spent the evening at the movies and took a short drive around town afterward. East of town, there was a powder house owned by the Hesson Hardware store. It was common in those days for miners, ranchers and construction companies to use dynamite in their work, and it was stored at the powder house, away from town. As the moviegoers approached the powder house, they noticed Bob White sitting in his car. When he saw them, he sped off.

The following morning, Bob's wife, Kathryne, caught the eastbound train for New York with a large amount of money in her possession.

Mike Connis tried to find Louie Lavell. After looking all over town, he became suspicious and contacted the local sheriff, Joe Harris, who started a search of his own.

They knew Louie had leased a small ranch called the Ryan Place, located in nearby Secret Pass. Sheriff Harris drove out to the Ryan Place and discovered that the small cabin had burned to the ground the night before. All that was left in the smoldering ruins were a few pieces of metal and five empty, charred gasoline cans.

Two local boys were east of town hunting rabbits, near the powder house. They discovered a gray hat and two pools of dried blood. The hat belonged to Louie the Greek.

Sheriff Harris went back to the Ryan cabin the next day and sifted through the ashes. He found a belt buckle with the word "Louis" stamped on it, several charred bones and a burned dental plate. Lavell had false teeth.

Joe Harris returned to Elko. When he got to town, he noticed Bob White at a service station, filling his car with gas. He immediately went to the district attorney's office to obtain a search warrant, but by the time he returned to the station, Bob was gone. After searching around town, Harris realized White was not in town and issued a nationwide bulletin for his arrest. A warrant was also issued for Kathryne's arrest.

A week later, Kathryne was located and arrested in New York City before she could board the ship for Ireland. In her possession was an address for Bob in Chicago. The next day, he was located hiding in a bunkhouse and was arrested.

Sheriff Harris and his wife traveled by train to Chicago to bring Bob back to Elko. When they arrived, a large crowd was waiting at the train depot.

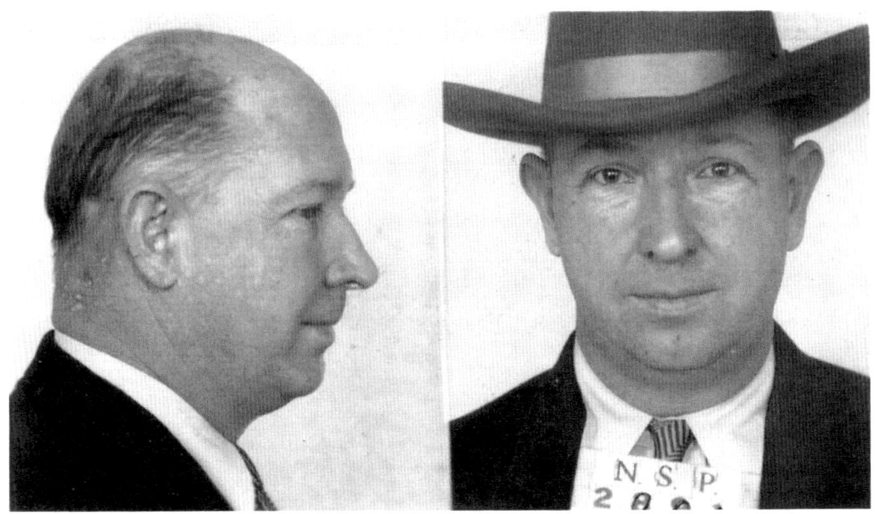

Booking picture taken of Bob White when he arrived at the Nevada State Penitentiary after his conviction. *Courtesy of Northeastern Nevada Museum.*

Any goodwill they felt for Bob White had evaporated; they were ready to hang him, right then and there. With help from his deputies, Harris was able to get White safely to the jail.

At White's trial, the jury found him guilty and sentenced him to die in the gas chamber at the penitentiary in Carson City. Nevada was the first state in the Union to use a gas chamber for executions; Bob White was the second person to die there.

There didn't seem to be any doubt in anyone's mind, because of the evidence, that Bob White was guilty. Sheriff Harris was one of the most respected people in Elko County. He served as sheriff of the large area for twenty-seven years and was well known for his good judgment, wisdom and common sense; he made very few mistakes. Sheriff Harris went to Carson City to talk to Bob just before the execution. He had just started the conversation when the warden came into his cell; Bob would not talk anymore. Sheriff Harris's daughter said years later, after her dad's death, that he was very upset about that incident. He believed that if he could have talked to Bob, he would have found out the truth, which he wasn't sure was brought out in the trial.

Did Sheriff Harris know something else? Was Bob White guilty? We may never know for sure.

18

METROPOLIS

A Ghost Town with No Gold

The name said it all. They called it Metropolis, which *Webster's Dictionary* defines as a large, important city or the center of great business activity. Although it was still in the planning stages, it would soon fit that description, or so the founders thought. The city, they said, would be very impressive, the largest between Denver and San Francisco, and the surrounding area would encompass miles and miles of productive farmland. A genuine Metropolis.

For a few years, it seemed it might fulfill that destiny. The Pacific Reclamation Company, a group of land developers from New York, knew of the successful farming projects in Fallon and Fernley, in western Nevada, where dams across rivers irrigated large sections of productive farmland. They envisioned doing the same thing in the eastern part of the state.

The developers bought forty thousand acres, plotted out streets for the town in the sagebrush and began work on the dam.

The dam would be fifteen miles east of the new city and fifteen miles northeast of the nearest railroad in Wells. A small stream, Bishop Creek, ran down a canyon into the surrounding sagebrush flats. A dam across the stream would impound water that would run into canals and irrigate the prospective farms on the flat.

Building the dam was a huge undertaking. Patrick J. "P.J." Moran of Salt Lake City, Utah, was hired as the general contractor for the job. Born in Yorkshire, England, he had been a stowaway on a ship headed for America when he was fourteen years old. He spent the next twenty years in the eastern United States, learning the building trades. Hearing of a need for his type of

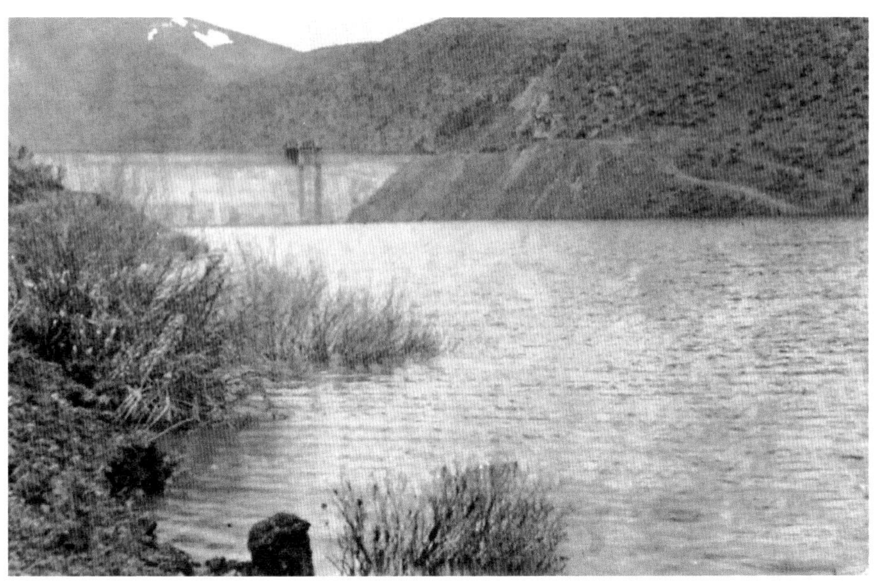

The dam in Bishop Creek Canyon before the lack of water rights prevented further use of the dam. *Courtesy of Northeastern Nevada Museum.*

work, he moved to Utah, where he built a successful construction company. He was forty-seven years old when Pacific Reclamation Company hired him to build the Bishop Creek Dam in Metropolis.

There was no road to the site, and all transportation between Wells and the dam was done with horse teams and wagons. After constructing the road, work began on a camp for the three hundred workers and more than one hundred horses and mules. Bunkhouses, a cookhouse, stables, corrals, a warehouse, a blacksmith shop, a store and, of course, a saloon were all needed.

Work began in the spring of 1911; it took just over a year and cost $200,000. It required 250,000 cubic yards of earth fill, masonry rubble and reinforced concrete. Some of the fill came from cleanup debris after the San Francisco Earthquake five years earlier. All supplies arrived in Wells by train and were hauled to the dam in wagons. The crews worked around the clock, using acetylene lamps at night. The key to dealing with the cold Elko County winter was more whiskey in the saloon.

Historians and engineers still marvel at the project. "I can't understand how he built it," said Bill Heyenbruch of the U.S. Corps of Engineers in Sacramento in 1973. "Even today with the latest technology, the task would be staggering. In 1911, it was something of a miracle."

Things did not end well for P.J. Moran. In spite of his amazing feat, he never received the $83,000 that Pacific Reclamation owed him. This created a serious financial setback, from which he never completely recovered.

While construction of the dam was progressing, things started happening in the new town. Streets were laid out and lots sold to eager folks who wanted to own a piece of the dream. The founders envisioned a city of seventy-five hundred people, and buildings started popping up in the sagebrush. An eight-mile spur from the nearby transcontinental railroad connected Metropolis to the world.

A large, elegant hotel was one of the first structures built. Constructed of brick and concrete, it was three stories high with a full basement. When finished by year's end, 1911, it was considered the finest such establishment between Ogden, Utah, and San Francisco. There were fifty guest rooms, thirty with their own baths, and every room had hot and cold running water. A thirty-two-horsepower diesel generator in the basement furnished electricity for more than 450 lights in the hotel and for all the other buildings in town. The surrounding farms still used kerosene lanterns and would not have electricity until 1958. All the hotel rooms were steam-heated from a large boiler in the basement. There was an electric elevator and central vacuum system.

More than three hundred people attended the grand opening of the hotel, including dignitaries, politicians and the press from all over northern

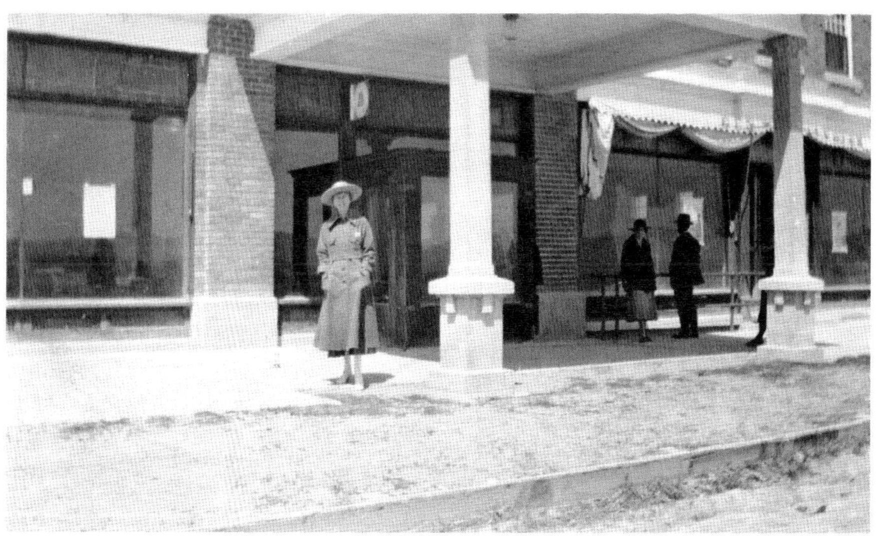

Eleanor "Hazy" Hasenkamp, standing in front of the abandoned hotel in Metropolis. *Courtesy of Wells Rural Electric Company.*

Nevada and nearby Utah. The *Elko Daily Free Press* stated it was the place to be in Elko County on that evening. A chef from Atlanta, Georgia, prepared the large banquet, after which guests danced into the morning hours.

The next building project in Metropolis was a large, two-story school. With eight classrooms and a gymnasium, it served more than 150 students during the peak years. The Metropolis High School basketball team would regularly beat teams from the surrounding area and even bested the University of Nevada once.

Students from the surrounding farms arrived in "school buses": canvas-topped wagons with benches on each side and steps in the back. A coal stove provided heat, and the driver sat near a window in front, with small slits underneath for the reins to the team of horses. Wheels and sleigh-runners were interchangeable, depending on the weather. Each wagon held thirty students and was pulled by a two- or four-horse team. The longest run was one hour from school.

Audrin Hyde Knudsen, who spent most of her life on a ranch near Metropolis, drove one of the wagons. One day, some children were playing around her wagon as she waited in front of the school to pick up the departing students. A noise frightened the horses, and they started running. She kept them on the road, and several older boys, on horseback, caught up with the runaway wagon and stopped the team. There was no damage to people or property.

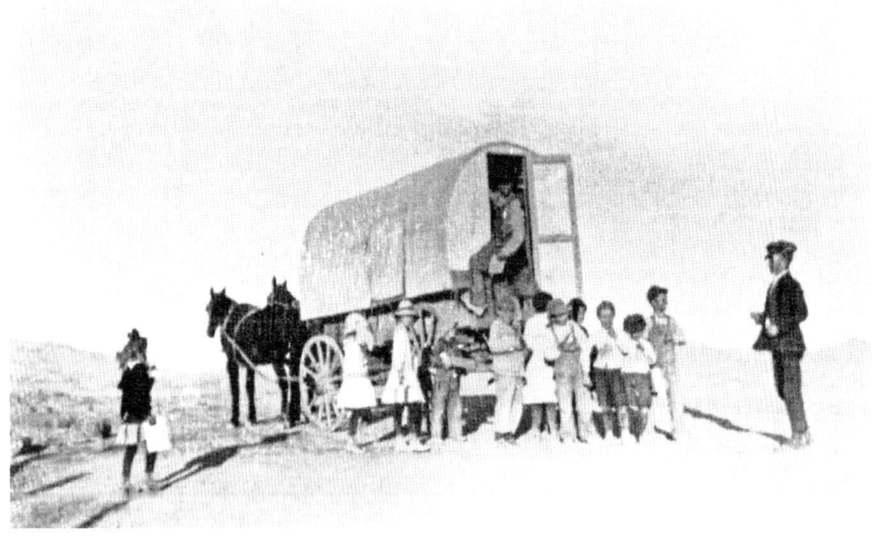

A Metropolis school wagon. *Courtesy of Northeastern Nevada Museum.*

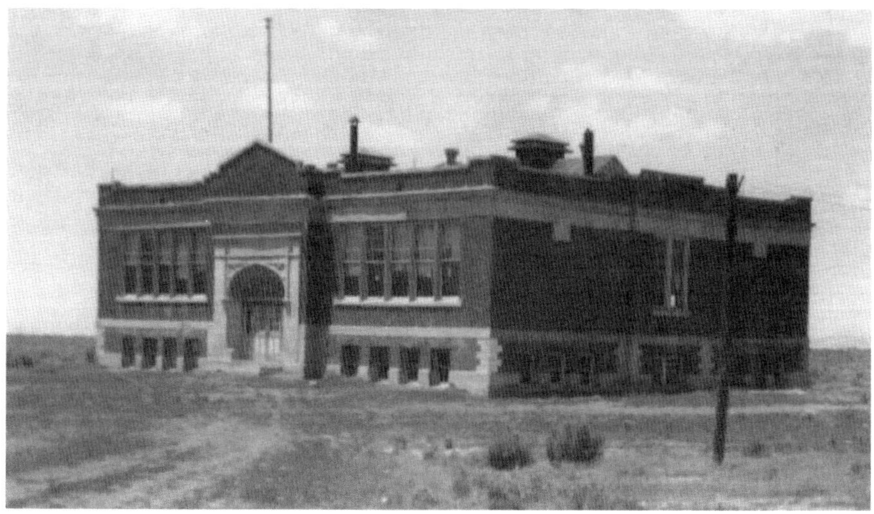

The school in Metropolis. *Courtesy of Northeastern Nevada Museum.*

Metropolis was the success story of the century, and many thought it would become the Elko County seat.

Then things started to fall apart. Within the year, farmers in Lovelock, 250 miles down the Humboldt River, reminded the Metropolis developers that water rights on Bishop Creek had been allocated to Lovelock years before; farmers upstream weren't allowed to use any of the water. Metropolis residents then tried dry farming. This worked for a few wet years, but several seasons of drought doomed that, too. Invasions of crickets and then rabbits destroyed what was left of the crops; people began to move away.

The hotel closed in 1913, but the building was still used as a community center for dances and parties. Service on the railroad spur was cut to one weekly freight train, with no passenger cars. Transportation for people was by automobile, over roads that were not well maintained.

Students continued to attend school, but not in the beautiful building they once had; it had been condemned due to leaks from a faulty roof. The first schoolhouse, built earlier, was put back into service. It was in a state of disrepair, and wind and snow blew through the cracks in the walls. The remaining students and four teachers bravely carried on.

Eleanor Hasenkamp, known as Hazy, was one of the schoolteachers. She arrived in Metropolis in 1917, after the glory years. She was very observant, and there was enough left in town for her to document the history as the town died away.

The school building had a stage, and the school produced many plays and other forms of entertainment. Hazy later said their productions were far superior to anything Wells ever tried. They occasionally loaded actors, costumes and scenery in cars and took the plays on the road to perform in Wells and Elko.

Teachers lived in a four-room teacherage. The building wasn't much, but they had beautiful furniture from the abandoned hotel. With no power generator in the hotel, the town went back to more primitive living conditions, without electricity. The teachers nailed a box to the outside of the house for a refrigerator in winter to keep meat cold or frozen. It attracted so many coyotes, which could smell the meat but couldn't get to it, that the teachers finally had to abandon that idea.

The few farmers left in the area had several good years raising potatoes. Teachers dismissed school for two weeks during harvest so the students could help on the farms. Teachers joined in, and Hazy later reported she was so stiff and sore after days of bending over and picking up potatoes that she wasn't sure she would ever recover.

In 1918, the great influenza epidemic hit the country, and Hazy was one of the unfortunate ones to contract the disease. It was nearly always fatal, but her fellow teachers nursed her back to health, and she survived.

Hazy taught in Metropolis until 1922 and left a written history of many fond memories of her time spent in the declining town.

The Great Depression was disastrous for the few people left in Metropolis. The hotel burned in the 1930s, and the school and post office were eventually closed. The railroad abandoned the Metropolis spur. Most of the farmers realized it was not a good area for farming and moved away or became cattle ranchers.

There are a few things of the grand scheme of Metropolis left today. The crumbling dam is still in the canyon, but it holds no water. The vault of the bank in the hotel and the entrance arch of the high school remain as lonely silhouettes in the sagebrush. Bricks from the school were salvaged and used to build a hotel in Wells. Descendants of the early settlers still hold reunions, and many of them are or will be buried in the cemetery, the only other thing left in Metropolis.

A question remains: did the developers really think it could succeed, or was it a scam? Some folks think the people in Lovelock knew what was going on but waited until after the dam was built. We may never know.

19

DAVE DOTTA

The Real Mayor

David Dotta was born in 1887 on the Adobe Ranch, twelve miles north of Elko. He was never very big in stature, but he made a big impact on the town of Elko, where he lived all of his adult life and spent thirty-four years as the mayor.

Dave's father, Emilio Dotta, was a very astute businessman. Through his many good investments, Dave was able to live a pleasant life, with time for the community service that he loved. Dave was his father's business partner for many years and was equally successful.

Emilio was born in Switzerland and came to this country in 1876 at age twenty-three. He went first to California, then to Eureka, Nevada, and finally to Elko County. He worked for wages and saved enough to buy a small freighting company. At age thirty-two, he returned to Switzerland and married Ercolina Dotta. She had the same surname as Emilio, but they were not related. Dotta is a very common name in Switzerland.

The couple returned to Elko County; within a year, Emilio had saved enough money to purchase the small Adobe Ranch. This is where Dave was born. The Dottas paid $2,600 for the ranch. Through hard work and many improvements, they sold the ranch six years later for $12,000 and purchased a larger one on lower South Fork River where it runs into the Humboldt River. Following the same work ethic, Emilio sold it a few years later at a profit and moved his family to Elko. There he established a brickyard, a coal yard and a lumber yard; financed ranches; and invested in rental property. Dave worked alongside him and gained a solid knowledge of good business practices.

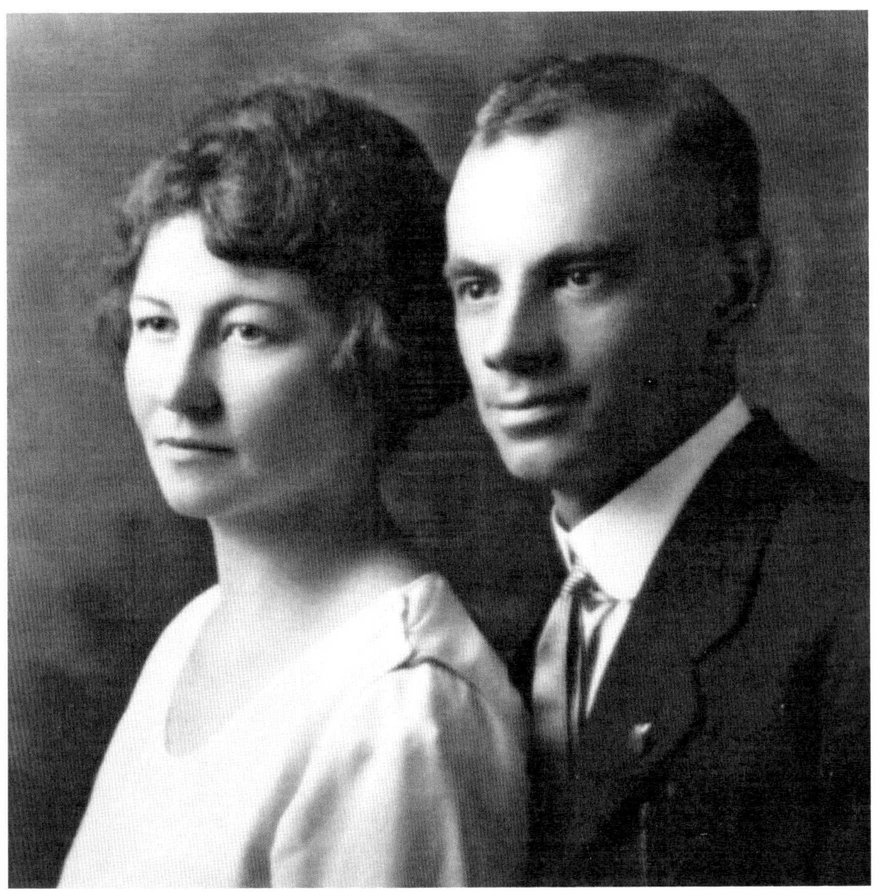

Dave and Rosa Dotta on their wedding day. *Courtesy of Northeastern Nevada Museum.*

Dave graduated from Elko County High School in 1907, where, despite his diminutive stature, he was a member of the football team. He attended business school in San Jose, California, and, in 1921, married Rosa Sperlich from Carlin.

Emilio and Ercolina retired and moved to California in 1922, and Dave took control of all these successful businesses.

His first taste of politics was in 1921, when he successfully ran for the Elko Board of City Supervisors, now known as the Elko City Council. There was fierce opposition at the time against the purchase by the city of the old China Ranch, near town. Dave was solidly in favor of the purchase, and it proved a good decision. The land was used for the city park, the first golf course, ballparks, the Elko County Fair Grounds and, eventually, Elko City Hall, the Northeastern Nevada Museum and the Elko Convention Center.

Dave became the fourth mayor of Elko in 1929, a position he would hold until 1955. He continued the city's plan of buying land for later development. The nation had not recovered from the Great Depression, and city money was scarce, but the Dottas felt it was important for the city to own the land surrounding the Hot Hole near the Humboldt River, outside the city limits. This parcel of land included a swimming pool, the only one in town. Rosa bought the entire property and sold it to the City of Elko for easy monthly payments of seventy-five dollars. The property provided a place for people to swim for the next fifteen years, until the city built one in town.

Many exciting things happened during Dave's terms as mayor. The singer and actor Bing Crosby owned a number of ranches in Elko County in the 1940s, and he and his family became familiar figures around town. Locals treated them just like regular folks, which is the way they wanted it. Dave and Bing became good friends.

In 1948, the City of Elko made Bing the honorary mayor, a position he held until his death in 1977. During the ceremony, Mayor Dotta presented him with a large, ornate key to the city. He told Bing it really wasn't necessary to have a key, because everything in the city was wide open.

During his Elko County years, Bing was on a hunting trip in western Canada and arrived at a hotel, dirty and disheveled after a day in the field. The hotel clerk refused him a room because he thought he was a vagrant. The Levi Strauss Company heard this story and made Bing a denim tuxedo to wear at times like this to look more respectable. The company also made one for Dave Dotta. A label inside each tuxedo read, "Levi's Tuxedo. Notice: to hotel men everywhere. This label entitles the wearer to be duly received and registered with cordial hospitality at any time and under any conditions. Presented to his honor, Bing Crosby, Honorary Mayor, Elko Nevada." The label in Dave's tux read, "Presented to his honor, Dave Dotta, Mayor." Both labels were signed by D.J. O'Brien, president of the American Hotel Association. Dave wore his on many occasions, and both tuxedoes are currently on display at the Northeastern Nevada Museum in Elko.

Bing donated money to many local charities, and when his movie *Here Comes the Groom* was released, the grand opening premiere was in Elko, at the Hunter Theater. The town overflowed with dignitaries and movie stars for several days. Not only the stars in the movie but many other Hollywood friends joined the celebration as well. The governors of both Nevada and

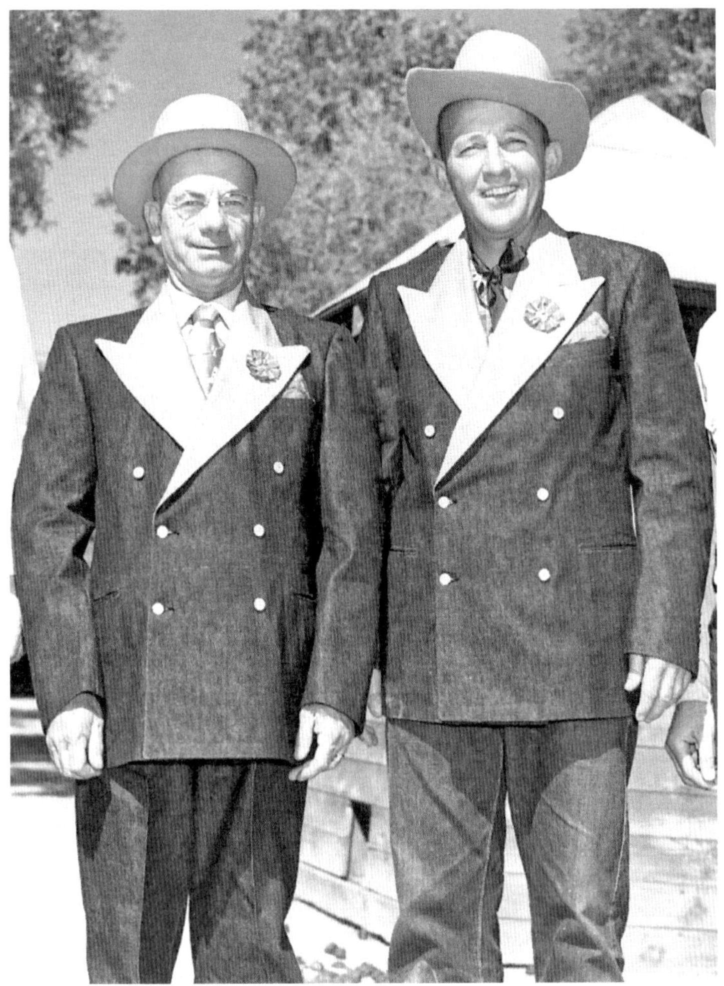

Elko mayor Dave Dotta and honorary Elko mayor Bing Crosby in their denim tuxedos, furnished by Levi Strauss Company. *Courtesy of Northeastern Nevada Museum.*

Utah were on hand, as were members of the Nevada congressional delegation. It was an exciting time for the people of Elko County.

Most of the citizens of Elko appreciated what Dave accomplished as mayor, as witnessed by the fact that he was reelected eight times. Mel Steninger, publisher of the *Elko Daily Free Press*, wrote this about Dave.

> *The secret of Mayor Dotta's accomplishments was that he treated the mayor's post as a full-time job even though it only paid a part-time salary.*

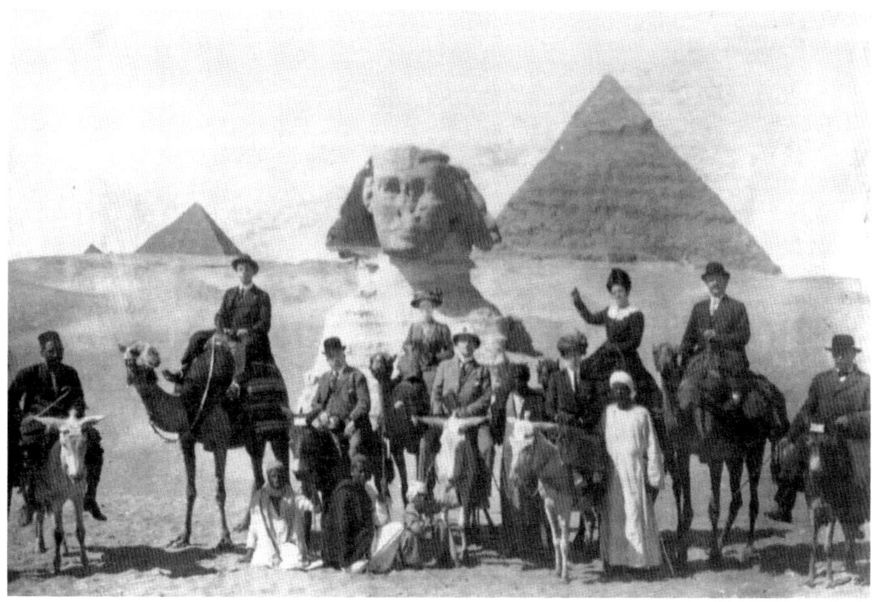

Dave and Rosa Dotta on a trip to Egypt. Dave (*left*) is on a camel, and Rosa is on horseback, waving. *Courtesy of Northeastern Nevada Museum.*

> *He could afford to do it because he had inherited wealth, but even under those circumstances, I don't think most people would have given as much time to community service as he did.*

Rosa, a graduate nurse, was involved in charitable work, especially in Carlin, where she grew up. During World War I, she established an emergency hospital there and cared for the troops stationed to guard the railroad tunnels and bridges in Carlin Canyon from sabotage. She was an accomplished horsewoman and was active in many local organizations.

After Dave was no longer mayor, the Dottas traveled extensively. They visited all fifty states and most of the countries in Europe. They spent time in the Middle East, Africa, Japan, the Philippines, Cuba, Mexico and Canada.

Rosa died in 1972, at age seventy-eight, and Dave in 1975, at age eighty-seven. Old-timers fondly remember Dave and Rosa for all the good both of them did for the community. The feelings were mutual. After all their travels, the Dottas said they never found any place in the entire world they would rather live than Elko.

20

Dan Murphy

The Soap Opera

Dan Murphy was a true pioneer in nearly everything he did—and he did some pretty amazing things. But for true "soap-opera" stories, he couldn't hold a candle to his descendants.

Born in 1825, Dan was a teenager in the third emigrant party to cross the future state of Nevada in 1844. The first two wagon trains made it with no loss of life but sacrificed many wagons and most of their possessions. This group, the Stephens-Townsend-Murphy Party, made it, not only with all members alive and well, but with all their possessions as well. They would go down in history as one of the most successful wagon trains to traverse the California Trail. They were not only the first emigrant party to do this successfully; it turns out they would be one of the last.

During the trip, the group camped one night at the site of present-day Halleck, in Elko County. Young Dan was not impressed—he wanted to get to California—but years later, he came back and made Halleck the headquarters of his many far-flung ranches.

At one time, Dan Murphy would own many ranches in Elko County, in addition to ranches in New Mexico, Arizona, California, Mexico and Idaho. He was one of the largest landowners in the world. He maintained a residence in Santa Clara for his wife and children, but he lived in Halleck. He was a devout Irish Catholic, generous to a fault and would lend a helping hand to anyone who needed it. A large, burly man, he fit the description of "Cattle King." He was well liked and well respected in Elko County.

Dan married Mary Fisher, who was of Spanish descent, and the couple had six children. Four died at an early age, and his only daughter, Diana, was his favorite. Because she was beautiful, with a fiery temperament, and the daughter of one of the wealthiest men in the West, she could have had her pick of men, but she fell in love with Morgan Hill. He was a bank teller and clothes model for a prestigious men's clothing store. He drove a fancy buggy pulled by a team of fine trotting horses and was an elegant dresser; he cut a wide swath in San Francisco society. He was eleven years older than Diana. Dan Murphy, of course, detested the young dandy and forbade Diana to see him. Diana and Morgan were secretly married, and Dan Murphy never knew, because he died just a few years later, in 1882, at the age of fifty-seven.

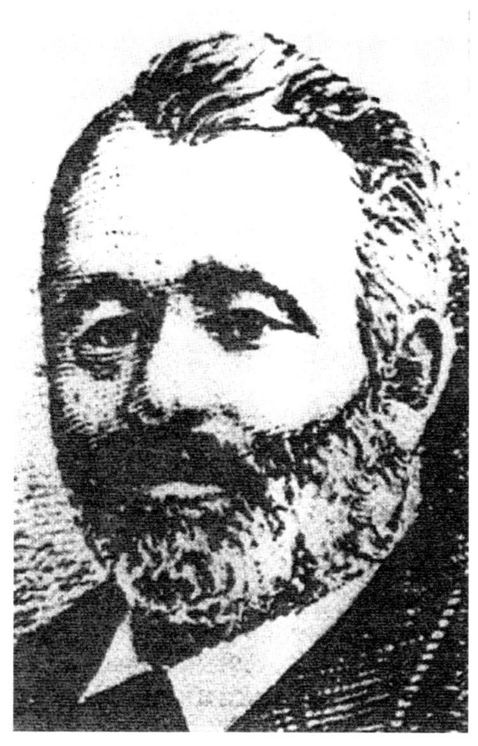

An unknown artist's conception of Dan Murphy. From *Elko Daily Free Press*. *Courtesy of Northeastern Nevada Museum.*

When the secrecy and intrigue were gone, Diana lost interest in Morgan but remained married to him. They built a lavish home in what would become Morgan Hill, California, named after its first citizen. They had one child, a daughter, Diane Murphy-Hill. Her name, except for one letter, was identical to her mother's. This caused a great deal of confusion. Their lives took different paths when Morgan decided he was tired of high society and went to Nevada to manage the ranches left to Diana by her father. She, on the other hand, craved more excitement and high society. She took their daughter and moved to Washington, D.C. Ever the socialite, she divided her time between Washington and San Francisco. Morgan, the man Dan Murphy thought was not good enough for his daughter, took over and successfully managed his vast ranches in Nevada. He established his headquarters at the Rancho Grande in northern Elko County and threw himself completely into ranching.

Young Diane was an unhappy child. She was very spoiled and even more beautiful than her mother. Very well educated, she spoke four languages: English to her father, Spanish to her mother and grandmother, French to the maid and German to the cook. She did not like the social life her mother was so fond of. Although she always stated she would marry a simple farmer, at age twenty-seven she married a Frenchman, Baron Hardouin de Reinach Werth, whose family had a ranch in western Canada. The elaborate wedding took place at St. Matthew's Cathedral in Washington, D.C. At Diane's request, only four people attended: the bride, the groom and Morgan and Diana Hill.

The newlyweds sailed to Europe for a honeymoon. Diane suffered a mental breakdown while in London and jumped from the hotel window to the cobblestone walk, eighteen feet below; she died instantly.

Shortly after this tragic event, Morgan Hill, who had morphed from a dashing socialite to an eccentric old man, suffered a stroke. Diana traveled to Elko and, to everyone's surprise, stayed there and took care of him for a year until his death in 1913. He was buried in Santa Clara next to his father-in-law, Dan Murphy.

Diane's husband, Captain Werth, as he came to be known in Elko, traveled to northeastern Nevada and assisted Diana in managing her father's

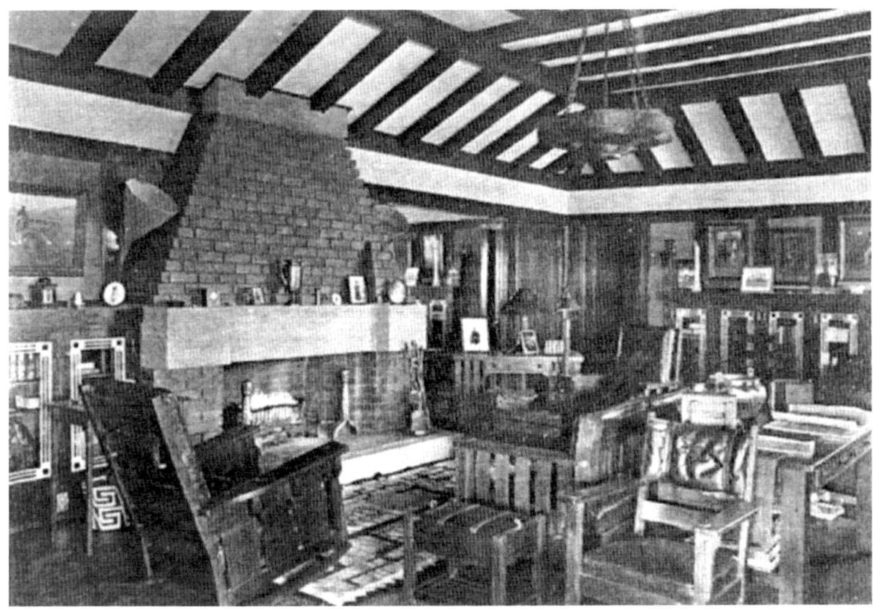

The living room of the Mira Monte house in Elko, 1914, where Diana Murphy Hill and Captain Werth lived. *Courtesy of Northeastern Nevada Museum.*

ranches. Diana built an impressive ten-thousand-square-foot home on Court Street in Elko. She lived in half of it, and Captain Werth lived in the other half. The people of Elko thought their living arrangement was "bold," but the still-beautiful Diana loved to entertain in a lavish manner. The shocked neighbors attended her parties with relish, even though they didn't approve. The large house Diana built in Elko is still there, owned by a local family.

Captain Werth was as successful at running the ranches as Dan Murphy and Morgan Hill had been. However, at the outbreak of World War I, the French government called him back to fight in the army. His friends in Elko never heard from him again.

Diana eventually sold the Elko County ranches and her fancy house on the hill and moved to London, where, at the age of sixty-three, she became the grand lady she had always dreamed of. She married Sir George Rhodes and became Lady Diana Rhodes. Her husband died two years later, and she spent her remaining years at the gambling tables of Monte Carlo, using money from the sale of the remaining Nevada properties. She died in 1937 at the age of seventy-eight.

21

Fannie Boyd

Does This Tent Remind You of Fifth Avenue?

Fannie Boyd lived in Elko County for only one year, but she was part of the early military history of the area. The story of the trials she endured during that year showcases not only what a strong, courageous woman she was but also what life was like on the new frontier.

She was born Frances Ann Mullen into a well-to-do family in New York City in 1848 and never ventured far from home during her first twenty years. In 1868, she married Orsemus Bronson Boyd, a recent graduate of West Point. Orsemus was a second lieutenant in the Eighth Cavalry; two days after their marriage, the army sent him to Camp Halleck, later named Fort Halleck, in Elko County, Nevada.

At that time, it was a very primitive place, miles from anywhere, and for lack of proper buildings, most of the enlisted men lived in dugouts in the side of a hill. The officers lived in tents. It did not seem to be a good idea for Fannie to follow Orsemus to Nevada, but she could not be swayed.

She left New York by ship in the middle of January, traveled across Panama by railway and went on to San Francisco by ship, arriving there three weeks later. Fannie said Panama was the most pleasant part of the trip.

She traveled by steamer to Sacramento and then by stagecoach to Virginia City. The road over the Sierra Nevada Mountains was treacherous in winter, and she later said there were many times on that portion of the trip when she thought she was going to die.

From there, it was not so frightening, but the stage was filled to overflowing with fellow passengers; for five days and nights, it was impossible to sleep.

The barely edible food available at far-flung outposts didn't make the journey any better. It was slow traveling, as recent warm days had melted the snow and the roads were terribly muddy.

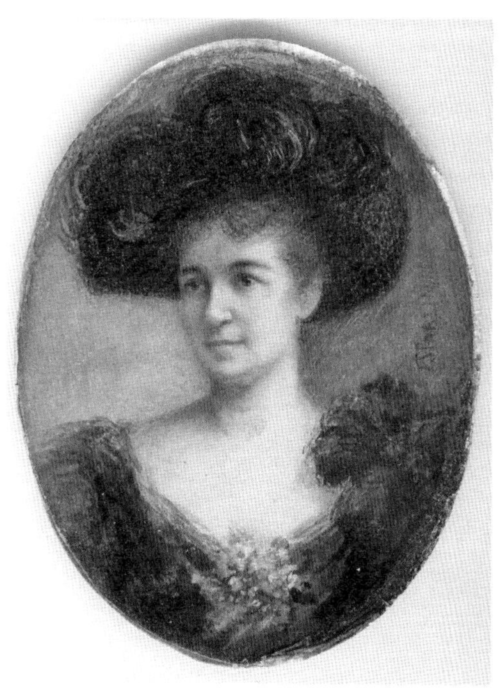

Fannie Boyd. *Courtesy of Jeffrey Howard Boyd.*

The stage route took her to Fort Ruby, about one hundred miles south of her new home, but her husband knew she was coming and met her there. Fort Ruby had been in existence for more than six years, and the Boyds took advantage of the fairly nice quarters. They spent two days letting Fannie recover from all those sleepless nights on the stage.

As there was no stagecoach service to Camp Halleck, they had to travel in an army ambulance pulled by mules. It was even more uncomfortable than the stagecoach had been, but it did not travel at night. The first night out, they slept in the ambulance on rough benches. The next two nights, they stayed in small cabins, shared with a dozen men. They fastened a curtain around their bed for some degree of privacy.

During the last night of the trip, a foot of snow fell. The next morning, the ambulance slid off the road. In attempting to get it out of a deep gully, the mules pulled the front wheels off the wagon. After a time, another wagon came along, but it had no top. They spent the last eighteen miles of their journey in a blizzard, wrapped in quilts to keep from freezing. Fannie's entire trip cost the Boyds $500, which was more than a month's pay for Orsemus.

She thought the worst was behind her and looked forward to her new home, which she pictured to be as beautiful as West Point, the only other army post she had ever seen. The primitive camp was quite a shock to her, but the worst part was her new living quarters. It consisted of two tents pitched together. Each was eight feet square, one serving as the living room and the other as a bedroom. Barley sacks covered the dirt floor. There were no windows to let in light.

The Boyds procured a large stove, which they put in the living room tent, and built a fireplace in the bedroom tent. The bed took up most of the space, so they had to be careful not to set their clothes on fire. The tent would regularly catch fire, and they spent much of their time patching burn holes.

At home, Fannie's family always had servants; she had no idea how to cook or wash clothes. Several soldiers felt sorry for her and helped her learn to do these chores.

Because of his West Point training, Orsemus was not popular at the camp; most of the men resented him. Life on the post was hard enough without having to endure these problems. Pay was in greenbacks, but they needed gold for everything they bought. The conversion cost them 50 percent, so they rarely had extra money.

Fannie bought dishes and cooking utensils from an officer at Fort Ruby and had them shipped to Camp Halleck. The rough wagon trip was not kind to the new acquisitions, and they arrived broken or bent out of shape. The Boyds needed chairs, so they sent to Austin for six chairs. Only one survived the trip. The teamster said they kept falling off the wagon and were run over.

Reading was one of the few pleasures in the isolated camp, and mail came once a week, but most books and magazines they ordered didn't arrive. They suspected someone up the line kept them for themselves.

The army furnished their food, but it was only bacon, flour, beans, coffee, tea, rice and sugar. When spring came, they were able to catch trout from nearby streams. In the summer, gardens at the camp provided bountiful crops, but because of the resentment toward West Pointers, the Boyds couldn't have any of it, even if they offered to pay for it.

During the summer, the men built barracks for enlisted men and cabins for officers, but the Boyds had to continue to live in their tents. In contrast to the winter, when the temperature often dropped below zero, summer was unbearably hot. There were trees on the nearby creek but none close to their tent to provide shade. There were gnats, wasps and rattlesnakes, and it was difficult to keep these intruders out of their tents.

The Boyds stayed at Camp Halleck for one year. When they left, they rode by team and wagon twelve miles to Halleck, where they met the newly completed transcontinental railroad. After waiting two days for a train, they boarded a freight car with rough seats, no windows and filled with railroad workers. After eighteen torturous hours, they finally got on a passenger car and traveled first class to San Francisco.

For the next eighteen years, Fannie followed Orsemus to many remote outposts in Arizona, New Mexico and Texas. Along the way, they had three children.

At the age of forty-one, Orsemus died during a campaign against Geronimo in New Mexico. Fannie, a thirty-seven-year-old widow with three small children, moved to New Jersey. At the urging of her friends, she wrote a book about her military experiences. Entitled *Cavalry Life in Tent and Field,* historians consider it one of the finest books ever written about life in military camps in the early history of the West. She looked back with some amusement at her first year as a military wife in the wilds of Nevada's northeastern frontier. She died in 1926 at the age of seventy-eight.

22

Tony Lema

The Day the Champagne Stopped Flowing

Anyone who follows the history of professional golf knows about the legendary Tony Lema. What most people don't know is that he spent part of his early career in Elko.

Upon his death in 1966 at the age of thirty-two, "Champagne" Tony was the fourth best golfer in the world, behind only Arnold Palmer, Jack Nicklaus and Gary Player.

Tony Lema was born in Oakland, California, in 1934, to parents of Portuguese descent. His father died when Tony was three years old, and his mother struggled to raise four children alone. Tony started playing golf on a small municipal course near his home at a young age, and many golfers, sensing his potential, assisted him with learning the game.

At age seventeen, Tony joined the U.S. Marine Corps and served in Korea. After his discharge in 1955, he obtained a job as the assistant golf pro at a San Francisco course. By 1957, he had developed his skills and qualified to be on the PGA Tour.

Later that year, Tony saw an ad seeking a golf pro at another small municipal course in Elko, Nevada. He answered the ad and was hired. The course, only three years old, was just a nine-hole facility. He spent one year in Elko and was well liked by the local golfers and everyone who knew him. His good looks and fun-loving personality made him a favorite wherever he went. Considered something of a playboy, he spent most of his time off the golf course at the local casinos, where he ran up large gambling debts. In a recent interview in the *Elko Daily Free Press*, Elko businessman Ted Blohm,

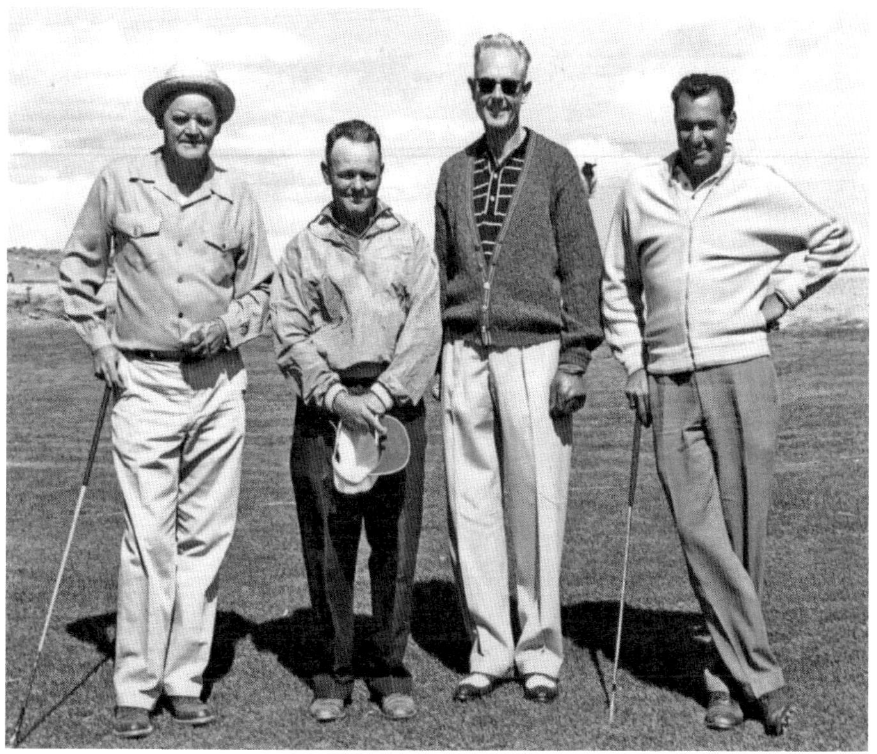

Tony Lema (*right*) with three other golfers when he was the pro at the Elko Municipal Golf Course, circa 1957. *Courtesy of Northeastern Nevada Museum.*

asked about Tony's time in Elko, said: "He and I were good buddies. He was single, I was single. We liked to do a lot of the same things—play golf, drink a little bit, chase girls. He was a really nice guy. I had a lot of fun with him." Bing Crosby, the famous singer and actor, had several ranches in Elko County, and he and his sons were avid golfers. Tony was good friends with the Crosby family.

In an effort to pay off his gambling debts, Tony went on tour during the next winter and finished in the top fifteen in eleven different tournaments. Realizing that he probably had a future on the tour, he called the City of Elko and resigned as the golf pro.

The next couple of years were not kind to him, and his winnings were meager. But in 1963, he met and married Betty Cline, an airline stewardess. He seemed to shake his playboy reputation, and his golf game improved.

Tony always had a good time when he played golf. People loved his joking manner, and according to his peers, he was probably the most well-liked professional golfer on the PGA Tour in the second half of the twentieth century. Pro golfer Johnny Miller said he was second only to Arnold Palmer in fan popularity. The media loved him, too. He acquired his nickname, Champagne Tony, at a tournament in Costa Mesa, California, in 1962, when he joked that he would serve champagne to the press if he won the next day. He did both. From then on, he always had champagne on ice waiting if he went into the last day of a tournament with a chance to win.

In 1964, he finished second to Jack Nicklaus at the Masters and won the Bing Crosby National Pro-Am at Pebble Beach. His greatest victory came later that year, when he won the Open Championship at the Old Course at St. Andrews, Scotland. He won by five shots over runner-up Jack Nicklaus. At the Firestone Country Club in Akron, Ohio, he won $50,000, the largest payoff in golf up to that time, during a matchup of the four major champions of the 1964 World Series of Golf. He played alongside Arnold Palmer, Ken Venturi and Bobby Nichols.

Over the next several years, he amassed an impressive record at professional tournaments. He won twelve official tour events, finished second at eleven events and placed third at four others. Tony was a member of the 1963 and 1965 United States Ryder Cup teams, a great honor accorded to only a few. His Ryder Cup record of nine wins, one loss and one tie is the best of anyone who ever played in multiple Ryder Cups. He finished in the top ten in eight of the final fifteen majors he played in. In 1963, *Golf Digest* named Tony the "Most Improved Player" for that year. He was on a path to stardom. His many fans in Elko avidly followed his successful career.

His great success on the golf course and his good looks made him a favorite on TV shows. He made a guest appearance on the TV series *Hazel* and appeared on the *Lawrence Welk Show*. Welk handed him the baton and had him direct the "Champagne Music Makers." Shortly before his death, Tony was interviewed on the national news by sports journalist Howard Cosell. Author Larry Baush wrote a book, *Uncorked: The Life and Times of Champagne Tony Lema*. Baush stated later, "Everybody loved him. He was quite a character."

On July 24, 1966, after finishing the PGA Championship at Akron, Ohio, in which he placed fourth, Tony and his pregnant wife, Betty, chartered a plane to fly to a tournament in Crete, Illinois, just south of Chicago. The twin-engine Beechcraft Bonanza, piloted by Doris Mullen, ran out of fuel less than a mile from their destination and crashed, ironically, on the seventh green of the Lansing Country Club Golf Course in Lansing,

Illinois. All four people on board died instantly. Tony was thirty-two, and Betty was thirty.

Dr. John Martin, a retired dentist in Elko and father of Brad Martin, the current golf pro at Ruby View Golf Course in Elko, remembered fondly the year Tony was the golf pro in Elko. John, who was eighteen years old at the time, worked at the golf course and caddied for Tony many times. In a recent interview in the *Elko Daily Free Press*, Dr. Martin recalled that Tony was a great guy and that it was fun watching what was going on with him. He added that Tony gave him lessons and was very nice to him. Martin said he remembered the day Tony died. He picked up the newspaper and saw the headline and just started to cry. It was one of the saddest days of his life.

Jim McKay, host of *Wide World of Sports*, reported on the tragedy. "The meat and potatoes are still on the PGA Tour," he said, "but the Champagne is gone forever. He was a good guy and a hell of a golfer."

23

Horace and Etta Agee

A Fighter and a Fiery Irish Lass

Horace and Esther "Etta" Agee were known for many things in their years in Elko County but mostly for his fighting side and her flaming red hair with the personality to match.

Horace's ancestors had been in this country since colonial days, and he was born in Nebraska in 1872. At age twenty, he came west and, although he had no money, was determined to become a cattle rancher. He spent some time in Colorado, where he and a friend got jobs hauling hay for a local farmer. When they finished, the farmer refused to pay them. Horace talked to a lawyer he knew, who advised him to steal the hay. Then the farmer would have to go to court to prove it was his hay and would not only have to pay the court costs but pay the boys as well. A neighbor who knew about the dishonest farmer loaned his wagon and a team, and the boys spent all night hauling the hay to another neighbor's place. They won their case and made enough money to continue on their westward journey. Unlike his usual methods, Horace did not have to fight for his money that time. Years later, Horace's good friend Milton Badt, who was eventually the chief justice of the Nevada state supreme court, was perusing a law book and came across a reference to that case in Colorado. He razzed his friend about stealing hay.

Horace acquired a freight wagon and four head of horses and eventually arrived in northeastern Nevada, where he worked for a number of years hauling freight to local mines.

He was a big man who loved to fight, and he was very good at it. He said he was afraid of no man; he wasn't even afraid of the devil himself.

Once while Horace was hauling parts to a mine for a new smelter, a copper spout fell off his wagon. When he realized it was missing, he rode back on one of the draft horses and found it along the trail. He managed to get the copper spout, which weighed more than 250 pounds, and himself back on the horse and rode to the wagon, carrying the spout. Amazingly, he did this all riding bareback.

The ancestors of Horace's wife, Etta, came to this country from Ireland. She was a true, flamboyant, Irish redhead. She and her widowed mother lived on a small place in Clover Valley; Etta herded the cattle, riding sidesaddle. While hauling ore from Spruce Mountain to the railroad, Horace went through Clover Valley. He attended a dance there one night and asked the lively redhead to dance. She was not impressed with Horace—in fact, she was engaged to someone else at the time. He started stopping more often, but she still wasn't interested, and neither were all her young friends. They did everything they could to discourage him; this only made him try harder.

He won Etta and her mother over when he defended them against a neighbor who was trying to steal their water. The judge in the case told him he could fight over the water but could not use any kind of weapon, even a shovel. He didn't need to. He vanquished the neighbor with his bare hands and won not only the fight but Etta's heart as well. They were soon married.

Horace and Etta lived in many different places in northeastern Nevada. Etta later told the story that they were the first in the area to have running water in their home. They lived in a tent, and every time it rained, the water ran in the front and out the back.

After several ranching ventures, the Agees acquired a large number of sheep and moved north to the O'Neil Basin, into the territory claimed by the O'Neil brothers, a rough bunch, not considered good neighbors. Everyone was afraid of them—except Horace Agee. The O'Neils sent one of their men to run Horace out of the country. When the man pointed a gun at him, Horace boldly walked up, grabbed the man's nose and twisted it so hard he dropped his gun. Horace told the man to go tell his bosses that if they wanted to get rid of him, they would have to send a *man*. Horace didn't have a problem with the O'Neils after that.

The Agees continued in the ranching business and acquired quite an empire. They built a big house in Wells, because they had eight children by then (two died at a young age). They moved for a short time to Oakland, California, so the children could experience city life but soon returned to Nevada.

Horace was always involved in politics. He served as the state tax commissioner and in the Nevada state legislature. He and Etta both served on the Elko County School Board, and he was the person most responsible for getting a new high school building in Wells in the early 1950s. He was instrumental in reorganizing the only bank in Wells and served as its president. He even ran, unsuccessfully, for governor.

Horace died in 1952. Mourners at his funeral included governors, senators, judges, wealthy men, ranch hands and sheepherders. He had arrived in Nevada with four horses and a freight wagon and left as one of the most respected members of the county.

After Horace died, Etta lived in Wells and spent a great deal of time traveling in her later years. She was a devout Episcopalian but loved horse races. A church member once asked her disapprovingly about her enthusiasm for the sport. Never one to back down, she replied, "If the Good Lord made draft horses to pull wagons and cow horses to work cows, didn't he make racehorses to race, so it would look pretty silly if nobody watched them."

Etta died in 1966 and was buried in Wells next to Horace. The fighter and his fiery Irish wife.

24

Jean McElrath

She Was Not "Handicapped"

The odds were against Jean, but in spite of suffering debilitating injuries at a young age that left her bedridden and blind for the rest of her life, she became a successful journalist, author and historian.

Jean Sybil McElrath was born on June 8, 1917, in Chloride, Arizona, a mining camp. Her father, Fenton McElrath, worked in a copper mine there. Her mother, Mabell McElrath, would play an important part in Jean's life as her caretaker and most ardent supporter.

When Jean was six weeks old, the family moved to Montana, where Fenton continued mining. In 1922, they moved to Cortez, Nevada, in Lander County, where he worked in a silver mine. Jean started school there in a small, one-room building, but she only spent one year there before the family moved to Wells. Her dad bought a garage there, and the family settled down to stay. Jean described the school in Wells as an overwhelming mob. There were approximately fifty students. Once she adjusted, she discovered what she would later describe as something seriously askew about herself: she liked school. She graduated from Wells High School in 1934 as the valedictorian of her class.

Her father died from an accident shortly after that, and Mabell raised her four children alone.

When Jean was sixteen, she fell off a hay wagon and injured her spine, which led to progressive rheumatoid arthritis. By 1938, she was unable to walk, and in 1950, at age twenty-one, she lost her sight. Despite many hospital visits and several surgeries, her health continued to deteriorate.

Mabell and Jean's sister Anita Cory, who lived in nearby Starr Valley, set up an "office" for her in the living room of the McElraths' home, and Jean started writing. They had a special table made to fit over her bed, and here she had a telephone, tape recorder and her trusty typewriter, affectionately named Simon, as in Simon Legree (the antagonist of Harriet Beecher Stowe's novel *Uncle Tom's Cabin*). Mabell and Anita helped with proofreading, research and re-typing. Anita, a photographer, added pictures to Jean's articles.

Jean had a friendly, outgoing personality, and many people would visit her, telling stories and reporting things going on around town and the surrounding area. She had an entertaining way with words, and soon her stories found their way into a weekly column in the *Wells Progress*, the local newspaper. Her reputation spread. In addition to writing stories, she became a news correspondent for the *Elko Daily Free Press*, the *Nevada State Journal* in Reno and the *Salt Lake Tribune* in Salt Lake City, Utah. Friends would call her with the latest news story, and she would call the newspapers and get her story in, often "scooping" other reporters. Years later, her obituary reported that her ability as a correspondent was legendary among editors.

There was a steady stream of people in and out of the McElrath residence. Everyone had a story, and everyone loved to visit Jean. She liked people and loved to "gab," as she put it. She spent a great deal of time on the phone, getting information for stories and talking to editors. She once said, "I am able to move my elbows, shoulders, and a few fingers—ah, yes, and my jaw!" The editor of the *Nevada State Journal* wrote, "She liked to write of the funny things best. She put a 'twist' in her pieces, of humor that often made the reader laugh aloud." In some of her autobiographical notes, she told a story of her attempt, later in life, to get her birth certificate. She wrote, "The State of Arizona

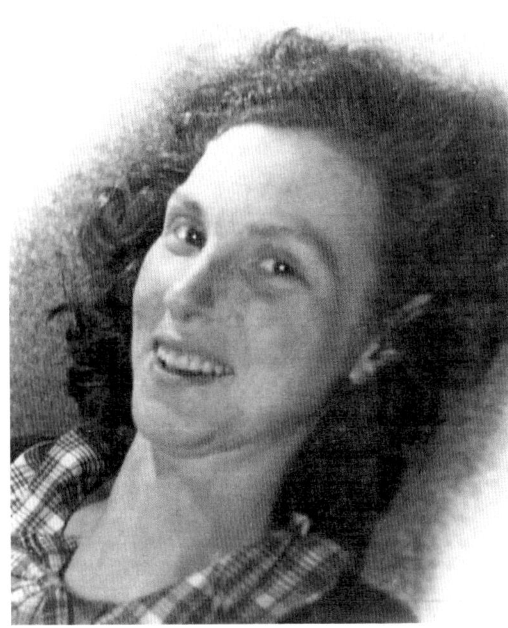

Jean McElrath. *Courtesy of Northeastern Nevada Museum.*

was so reluctant about conceding that I was ever born, I began doubting it myself. It took three years, the U.S. Bureau of Census, the Episcopal Church, Wells School District, my Mother's oath, $5.00, and a jillion or so letters to pry a 'Delayed Birth' certificate out of them...possibly a record for 'delayed birth.'"

Jean never complained about her situation in life. Many who read her stories but didn't know her had no idea she was bedridden and blind because of her visually descriptive and humorous writing style. She once commented, "When you hit a problem, you aren't going to stop and spend what little time you have moaning about what you can't help." Another time she wrote, "As for the word 'handicap,' it seems to me that to the person concerned, a handicap is pretty much a matter of attitude. It depends, too, I'd say, on what you are trying to do. Nearly everyone is handicapped in some way. Hardly anyone is handicapped in every way."

She wrote stories and articles for a wide variety of magazines and other publications, ranging from the *Western Livestock Journal* to the *Wall Street Journal*.

Because of the fondness the people in northern Nevada felt for her, she was made an honorary member of many organizations, including the Nevada Peace Officer's Association, Nevada Cowboys Association, Wells Chamber of Commerce, Northeastern Nevada Historical Society and Future Farmers of America.

In 1964, a number of historical short stories and vignettes written by Jean through the years were compiled into a book, *Aged in Sage*. It sold widely and is now a collector's item. The foreword of the book, written by famous Nevada author Robert Laxalt, said:

> *In this book, author Jean McElrath has done a remarkable thing. Not only has she breathed life into fine old stories that would otherwise have been left to die, but she has done so with a true storyteller's gift of narrative, with kindness, and a deep understanding of the people she writes about.*

Jean received many awards and honors during her life, but the highlight was in 1965, when she was named a Distinguished Nevadan, a prestigious honor, by the University of Nevada. She traveled to Reno in her sister's station wagon and received her award from her gurney. She received a congratulatory telegram that was eight feet, three and one-half inches long, signed by her many friends and supporters. It was second in length only to the telegram relaying the Nevada State Constitution to President

Abraham Lincoln in Washington at the time of Nevada's admission to the Union in 1864.

Jean died in 1967, at age fifty. Her extraordinary mother, who had been her caregiver for thirty years, died twenty-four years later.

Three years after Jean's death, a collection of twenty-seven years of her "Tumbleweeds" columns from the *Wells Progress* was compiled into another book, *Tumbleweeds, 1940–1967*, which helped preserve the history of northeastern Nevada. It has also become a popular collector's item.

25

Lewis Rice Bradley

They Called Him Broadhorns

They called him "Old Broadhorns," and the name seemed to fit. He was big and tough, and nobody messed with him. He eventually became the second governor of the state of Nevada, and it did not mellow him in the least.

He was born Lewis Rice Bradley in 1805 in Orange County, Virginia, where his ancestors had settled when they came from England in the 1700s. He never used his full name; he always went by L.R. He had very little formal schooling but always had a good head for business. His father died when L.R. was thirteen, and he took care of his mother and many siblings until they were grown.

He later moved to Missouri, where he met and married Virginia Willis. They had four children, but his wife died when the youngest was only six weeks old. The baby died a year later. After several years as a farmer in Missouri, he twice drove large herds of cattle to California and sold them to hungry gold rush miners and eventually acquired a ranch there. On one of these trips west, L.R. became very ill. One of his men, nineteen-year-old Jefferson Henderson, had studied pharmacology and gave his boss some drugs from the scant medicine bag he carried. Fearing he would die, L.R. gave the young man a letter and asked him to make sure his oldest daughter, Sarah, received it upon his death. After a time, L.R recovered, and they continued on to California. Henderson eventually returned to Missouri, looked up Sarah and gave her the letter. A romance ensued, and they were later married.

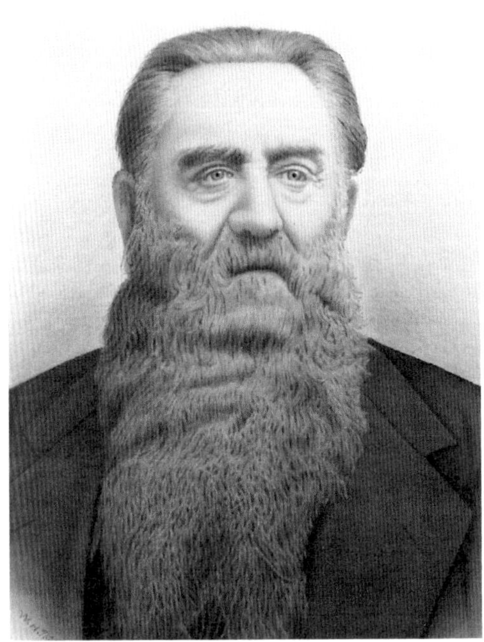

Lewis Rice "L.R." Bradley. *Courtesy of Northeastern Nevada Museum.*

L.R. and his son John Reuben, known as J.R., moved their cattle operation to the Nevada Territory. They went to Pershing County and then to Lander County and, in 1866, established a ranch in Mound Valley, Elko County. J.R. went on to Deeth, a few miles north, and was a prominent rancher there for many years.

The citizens of Nevada elected L.R. Bradley as governor on the Democratic ticket in 1870. As a rancher, he was an outsider in Carson City, the state capital, because most of the politicians of the day were miners. But he was firm in his convictions and would not be intimidated.

At one point, Bradley had a showdown with his lieutenant governor, Frank Denver. As was the custom, the lieutenant governor also served as warden of the state prison. The legislature passed a bill changing that, and Bradley appointed another man as warden. Denver, sensing his power and financial rewards slipping away, barricaded himself in the prison and refused to hand over his keys. Governor Bradley sent word to Denver that members of the militia would march to the prison and remove him, even if they had to kill him in the process. Denver evidently believed the governor and turned over his keys.

Bradley was reelected in 1874, but a battle with the miners doomed his try for a third term. Those with mining interests already paid less in taxes than other entities, and when the state legislature, made up mostly of miners, passed a bill reducing the tax on mining proceeds by another 30 percent, Bradley threatened to veto it. At the time, the governor's ranching interests in Elko County were suffering because of his absence, and a rich and influential miner, knowing of the governor's plight, approached him with a blank check and told him to fill in any amount he wished if he would not veto the mining bill. After Bradley tore up the check, he bodily threw the man out of his office and vetoed the bill anyway. Because of this, Bradley suffered the outrage of many citizens, most of whom depended on the mining industry for a living. One newspaper had a headline reading "Our Boss Lunatic," and another urged the legislature to conduct a commission, "*de lunatico equirendo*…and that pending the inquiry, pen and paper be carefully kept out of his way. In his hands they are as dangerous as a razor in the hands of a maniac."

L.R.'s other daughter, Virginia, was married in a splendid ceremony in the governor's parlor in Carson City to a young attorney, C.H. Belknap. He later became a justice of the Nevada supreme court. As L.R. never remarried, Virginia served as hostess for the social occasions held during Bradley's term as governor.

Daughter Sarah and her husband, Jefferson Henderson, who had saved L.R.'s life earlier, moved to Elko County in 1877 to assist the governor with his ranching operations. Jefferson didn't much care for ranching, and in 1880, he and Sarah moved to Elko, where he opened the Henderson Bank. He was honest, had a good head for business and built up one of the soundest banking institutions in the West. He handled large amounts of money for the people of Elko County, and his Henderson Banking Company served northeastern Nevada for many years. Jefferson and Sarah's son John followed in his father's footsteps in the banking business, and their son Charles became an attorney and a U.S. senator from Nevada.

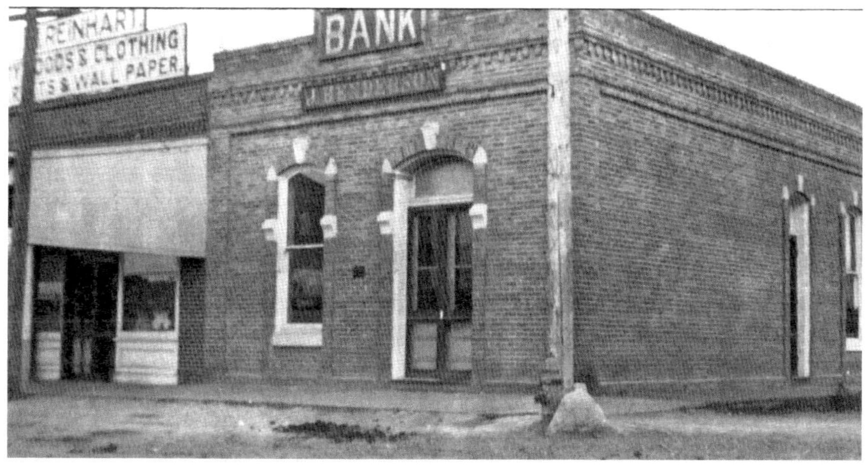

The first Henderson Bank building in early Elko, where Jefferson Henderson, son-in-law of L.R. Bradley, started a banking institution. *Courtesy of Northeastern Nevada Museum.*

During Bradley's tenure as governor, he persuaded the legislature to establish the first University of Nevada, in Elko. It opened in 1874 with only seven students and existed there for eleven years. Because of the remote location and difficulty traveling from the western part of the state, the school never had more than thirty-five students. In 1885, the university moved to Reno, where it remains today.

L.R. Bradley's defeat for a third term as governor was not his only setback. During the very severe winter of 1878–79, he lost thousands of head of cattle on his ranch in Elko County, his health deteriorated and he lost his bravado. He moved back to Mound Valley, frustrated and disappointed, and died several months later, in 1879. He was seventy-four. Although five other men from Elko County have since become governor of Nevada, Old Broadhorns was the only one to return after leaving office. He is buried in the Elko Cemetery.

26

Susie Raper

It's Hard to Convict a Pretty Woman

Susie Raper had many things going for her. She was young, beautiful, an accomplished horsewoman, a crack shot with a rifle and a fearless cattle rustler. But perhaps her greatest talent was convincing men, especially men on juries, that she was innocent, even when she was not.

There are many conflicting stories of her escapades through the years—all of them very entertaining. Susan Warfield was born in New South Wales, Australia, and some sources say she came to Nevada as a small child with her parents. Others pegged her arrival at a later age, with a husband and three small boys in tow. Most agree she married Thomas Raper when she was very young, possibly fifteen years of age, and they were the parents of three boys. One story claims Thomas was rich and owned the Yankee Mine at Downieville, California, and that Susie, as she came to be called, had married him for his money. Another version had the Rapers in Paradise Valley, north of Winnemucca, with a failing mine and no money. One way or the other, Thomas turned up dead. Susie claimed it was from an Indian attack and then changed her story to say he had deserted her and the boys and she didn't know how he died. Many people in the area thought she had murdered him. A letter, supposedly found at their home in Paradise Valley after she had moved on, was from Thomas to Susie. He said it was pretty hard for a man to leave his children forever on account of a damn thief. If all this was true, she may have already begun her life as a rustler.

She made her first appearance in Elko County in 1869, when she was twenty-nine years old. She had no husband and three small boys: Joseph,

Robert and William. Instead of taking in washing, like a respectable woman, she took to rustling cattle. She didn't do it alone—she always had men to help her—but apparently she was the boss, and they took their orders from her. She soon established a reputation. An ad in the *Elko Independent*, a local newspaper, stated:

> *Strayed from my ranch on the South Fork of the Humboldt River, near Shepherd's Station, about thirty head of American steers and heifers, branded with a circle "S" on the left side, and vented on the shoulder, and a small "s" on the hip. Mark-crop off each ear and two slits in the left. A liberal reward will be paid for information that will lead to their discovery, to be sent to my ranch or left at Reinhart's store in Elko.*
>
> *J.A. Shepherd. Elko, December 22, 1869*

Although no one knew what had happened to Shepherd's cattle, they certainly didn't suspect it was the work of a gang of cattle thieves led by a woman. However, Shepherd found his cattle, along with others, on a ranch in Pine Valley where Susie was living, and her antics soon became a local soap opera.

In all, she was arrested and taken to trial three different times in Elko County, charged with grand larceny. She was acquitted all three times. According to one of the jurors after a trial, "Verily it is hard to convict a woman." She was also arrested, tried and found not guilty of stealing $500 worth of jewelry from a local woman. No details are known about how this all happened. At one of her trials, she took two of her sons, ages nine and seven, to court with her. Her attorney used the fact that she was a poor mother just trying to care for her boys. It worked.

Her reputation spread, and local citizens would attend her trials to enjoy her latest scandalous escapades. In 1871, trying to outrun her bad reputation, she, along with a Captain Payne from Carlin, moved farther west, to Lander County, and then farther still to Humboldt County. After being accused and acquitted of continued cattle rustling, she relocated to Durango, Colorado, taking Captain Payne and her sons with her. She and Payne started a stage line to San Antonio, Texas, but when he ended up in jail, she immediately married Jack Yonkers and they left for New Mexico, leaving Payne still in jail.

The couple bought a bar in Socorro, New Mexico, but it didn't prosper. They moved out of town to a small cabin, where Jack died. Susie said he had smallpox and that she had to bury him all by herself, in an undisclosed location. The story was suspicious, as there had been no smallpox in the area for years, but the local lawmen were charmed by her and did not investigate.

Next, she met a wealthy rancher, George Black. As time went on, she gradually convinced him to put parts of his property in her name. Two days after she finally had title to his entire ranch, she shot and killed him. She told local officials Black had come at her with an axe and she shot him in self-defense. The sheriff was taken with her and refused to press charges, but the citizens of the area were outraged and insisted she be tried for murder.

Not much is known of her sons through all this, but two of them suddenly appeared and were going to testify for her. She managed to slip out of town just before the trial, leaving her sons to be arrested. One of them told the authorities many things about his mother's past, and he was released for cooperating with them.

Thinking she was safely away from the law in Socorro, Susie married Charles Dawson, but he was soon killed in a gunfight. She went to the authorities to have the men arrested who had murdered Dawson, but the sheriff thought it was self-defense and refused. However, the story was in the local paper. Authorities in Socorro read it and re-arrested her. She stood trial for George Black's murder. Her son finally testified against her, but as usual, she convinced the all-male jury of her innocence. The citizens of Socorro did not have the revenge they sought for her outrageous behavior.

The last anyone in Elko heard of Susan Warfield Raper Yonkers Black Dawson, she had gone to the Arizona Territory. She reportedly died in 1897. Citizens of Elko County had followed her antics through the years, after she left there, and were convinced that wherever she was, and whatever mess she managed to get into, she would probably convince a jury of her innocence. Some didn't believe she had actually died; they thought she would talk her way out of that, also.

27

Valentine Walther

The House that Valentine Built

Valentine Walther accomplished many remarkable things in his ninety-one years, but his greatest legacy was his house.

Valentine was born in 1842 in Germany, where he developed a love and knowledge of gardening. He, his father and a younger brother came to America when Valentine was seventeen, and his mother and the rest of the family came three years later. For the next ten years, they lived and farmed in New York, Ohio and St. Louis, Missouri. While there, Valentine became acquainted with Sophie Roeder, a former schoolmate from Germany who was also living in St. Louis with her family. Nothing came of the romance at that time, as Valentine soon went west and worked in a mine in Belmont, Nye County, in central Nevada. He worked there until he had enough money to buy land in Diamond Valley, north of Eureka, Nevada, where he established a dairy and raised beef cattle. Sophia came to Elko to visit family who lived there, and the two were reunited and married in 1870. The couple lived in Diamond Valley for six years, where they had four children. In 1876, they moved to Sherman, Huntington Valley, in southern Elko County, where they homesteaded six hundred acres. The first year the family lived in two covered wagons, and then Valentine built a small, two-room log house. The couple had eight more children—quite a crowd in two small rooms.

When their youngest child was five, Valentine and Sophie were traveling in a wagon hitched to a team of horses. As they approached a gate, Valentine got off to open it. Sophie drove the team through the gate, but one horse leaned to the side, and a portion of the harness caught on the fence post. That startled the team, and they headed down the road at a full gallop. Valentine ran after them but was unable to catch up. Sophie managed the team well, but a large hole in the road caused the wagon to come loose from the team. The tongue of the wagon was driven into the ground, which catapulted the wagon in the air and threw Sophie over the front of the wagon, about twenty feet. When Valentine caught up to her, she was unconscious and badly injured. He made her comfortable and walked back to the ranch to get another wagon and team to rescue her. After getting her home, he sent a messenger to Elko, almost sixty miles away, for a doctor. By the time the doctor arrived, she was up and walking around and seemed fine. Later she complained of chest pains and died that night. She was thirty-one years old and left her husband and twelve children.

Along with caring for the twelve children, Valentine spent most of the next two years building a very large home for his very large family. It had two stories plus a cellar underneath. Made of eighteen-inch pine logs, it had nine rooms on the main floor and one large room upstairs. He also built numerous outbuildings: a barn, a blacksmith shop, a creamery and, because he realized the importance of education, a schoolhouse. He hired a teacher, who lived at the ranch, to teach his children.

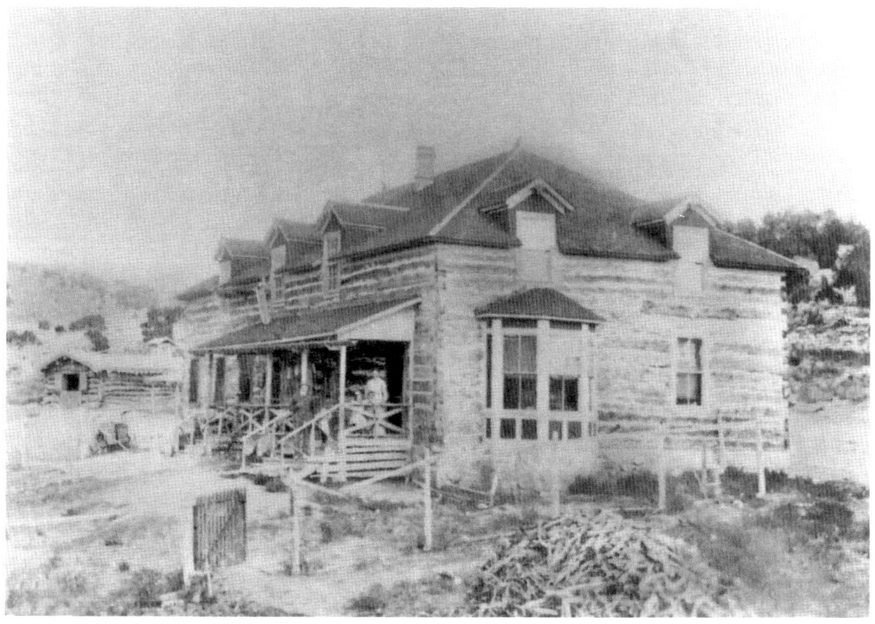

Valentine Walther built this house at Sherman, Huntington Valley, south of Jiggs. *Courtesy of Northeastern Nevada Museum.*

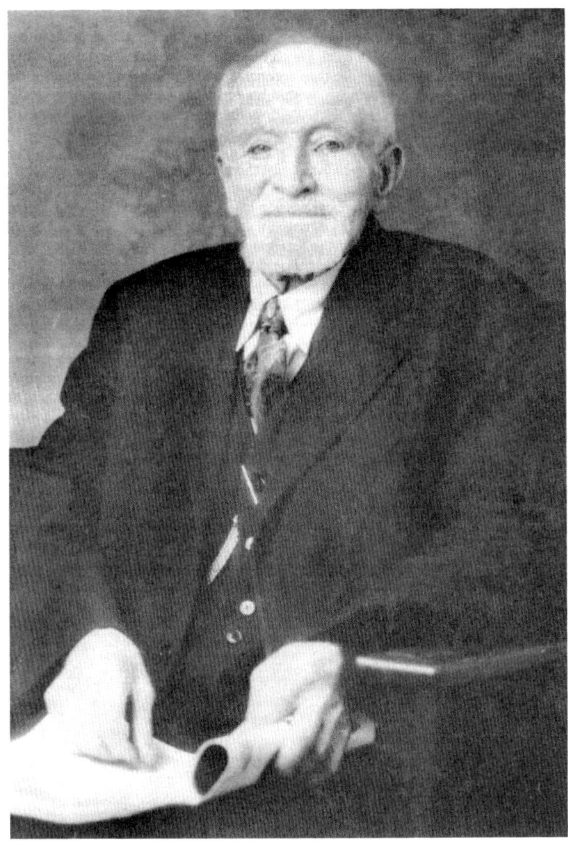

Left: Valentine Walther, shortly before his death in 1933 at age ninety-one. *Courtesy of Northeastern Nevada Museum.*

Below: Valentine Walther's house in 1997, moving through Elko to its location in the Elko City Park, where today it houses the Elko Area Chamber of Commerce. *Courtesy of Northeastern Nevada Museum.*

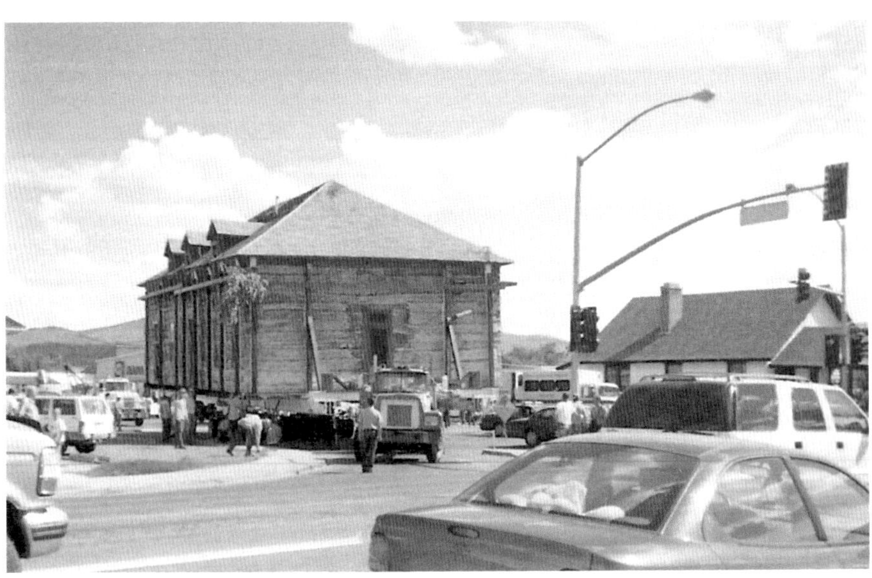

Valentine always retained his love of farming and had a fine garden and large orchards. In spite of the short growing season in Elko County, he raised asparagus, raspberries, strawberries, apples, apricots, peas, potatoes and other fruits and vegetables. He grew much more than his large family needed and hauled the rest, by team and wagon, to markets in Elko, Eureka and Tuscarora. The children assisted him in the gardens and orchards. In addition to cold weather, deer, rabbits and other small animals were problems, so he built miles of tall fences out of willows to keep them out of his gardens. He also made large amounts of sauerkraut, cheese and cottage cheese, which his family and all the neighbors enjoyed.

When Valentine was eighty years old, he sold the ranch at Sherman and moved to Elko, where he lived with some of his children. He spent his time puttering in their gardens and made showplaces of their homes. He also liked to trim trees for his family and neighbors and would often climb up into the trees. Because of his age, family members tried to discourage him from this pursuit, but he insisted, and although he fell out of trees several times, he was never seriously hurt. He loved to play cards and insisted on a game every night before he would retire. He died in 1933 at the age of ninety-one.

In 1997, a group of people in Elko acquired the large house in Huntington Valley and four of the surrounding outbuildings—the stable, creamery, blacksmith shop and schoolhouse—and moved them all to Elko. They reconstructed them in the Elko City Park, where the large house now serves as a visitors' center and home of the local chamber of commerce. The outbuildings contain historic items from the collections of the nearby Northeastern Nevada Museum. Every year, many people visit and enjoy the big, beautiful house that Valentine built.

28

Lillian Hansen

Paris, Rome, Florence...Elko

Elko was a very small town, located hundreds of miles from large shopping areas, but for more than three decades, the women of Elko County could wear the latest fashions from Chicago and New York and even Paris and London. They didn't have to travel to these places to purchase high fashion—they could buy it in Elko, at a store called Lillian's. The lady who owned it brought a touch of class to all those who frequented her dress shop.

Lillian Slatter was born in Brigham City, Utah, in 1905. She traveled to Elko in 1924 to visit a brother who lived there. She liked it so well that she stayed. Two years later, she married Delbert Holland, the son of a local rancher, but he died just nine years later. He was only twenty-eight.

Lillian went to work at the Seymour Jacobs Company, a local clothing store, where she was in charge of the ladies' dress division, the bookkeeping and decorating the store.

Lillian married again, this time to Harold Hansen, a supervisor for the Humboldt National Forest. They lived in Paradise Valley, north of Winnemucca, where his job was located. He eventually transferred to Elko, and Lillian was again back in her favorite town. Harold was the construction supervisor of the new Lamoille Canyon road and Angel Lake road, two important byways for traveling into the scenic Ruby Mountains.

With her experience in merchandising, Lillian was soon in demand at local clothing stores. She worked at JC Penney Company, the Tip Top Dress Shop and O'Leary's, a small ladies' apparel store on Idaho Street.

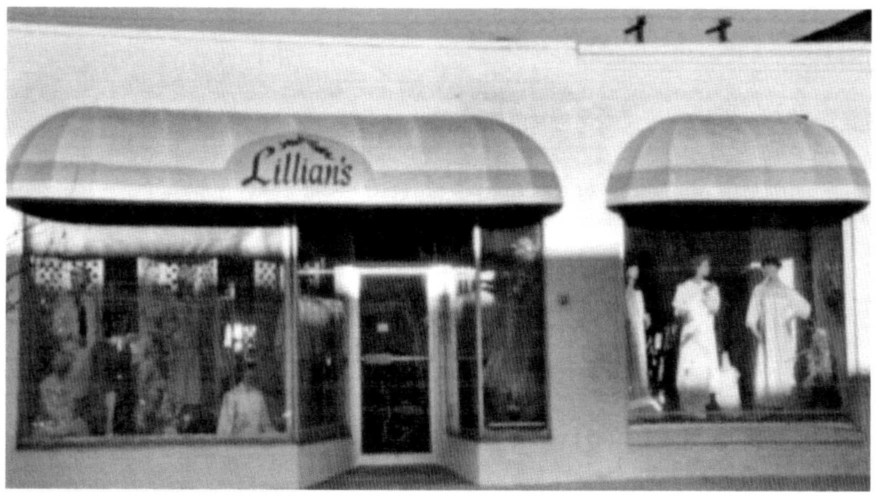

Lillian's dress shop in downtown Elko. *Courtesy of Northeastern Nevada Museum.*

Within a year, the owners of O'Leary's, realizing her merchandising skills and popularity in the community, asked her if they could change the name from O'Leary's to Lillian's. She agreed, and the next year, in 1949, she bought the business from them. Then it truly was Lillian's.

Several years later, Lillian bought another dress shop across the street from her store. The new one, Lass & Lady, was for teenagers, and Lillian's catered to women. She had both stores for eight years. Her husband, Harold, died in 1964 at age fifty-seven, and she sold the Lass & Lady business. Lillian continued her original dress shop, and the name "Lillian's" became synonymous with quality, style and service for well-dressed women in the area. It was located at 461 Idaho Street.

It was going to get even better. The owner of the building that housed her shop decided she needed a better place to operate from, so he tore down the old building and erected a new, larger store. She started traveling to Los Angeles, San Francisco and Denver to shop for new merchandise and then widened her scope to Scottsdale, Washington, Dallas and New York. She was bringing the latest national fashions to the ladies of Elko. Expanding from there, she began attending fashion shows, combined with buying expeditions, in Paris, London, Italy and Switzerland.

Her knowledge of buying merchandise and knowing how to display and market it proved to be an asset in her years in the business. She was very particular about the store's windows, with impressive mannequins and decor. She believed the windows were her "24-hour-a-day salespeople."

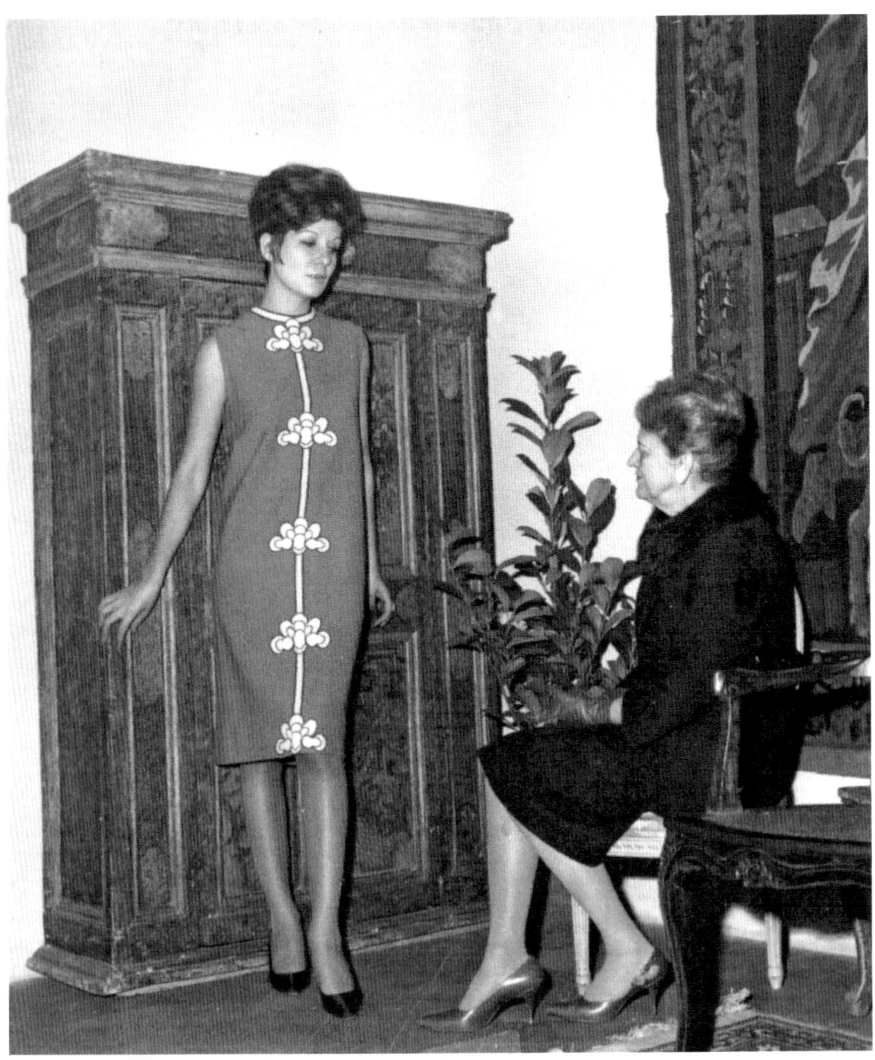

Lillian Hansen in Paris, France, on a buying trip for her dress shop. *Courtesy of Northeastern Nevada Museum.*

The years were not without problems, however. In addition to losing two husbands, there were issues with the actual building, even though it was quite new. On one occasion, a local friend opened the door to her shop and yelled, "Lillian, give me your books and records—your roof is on fire!" With help from the Elko Fire Department, many friends and other business owners, the inventory was removed. The only damage from the fire was to the building itself, which was soon refurbished.

Heavy rains would also cause water to run down the side of the building and in the front door. Once during a rainstorm, five sales girls formed a bucket brigade to dump water back onto the sidewalk. Occasionally the basement flooded, and the building owner and the fire department assisted in hauling and pumping the water out. The Elko City Street Department finally made some changes in the alley behind the stores on that block so that the rainwater would not flow through the window wells and into the basements.

On a cold January night in 1965, the JC Penney building at Fourth and Idaho Streets burned to the ground. Before the flames were controlled, it was feared the entire block would be destroyed, and Lillian's was one of those stores. Again, community members helped remove everything from all the stores on the block. The Stockmen's Hotel provided space for the entire inventory until the businesses could move back into their refurbished stores.

Lillian was very community minded. She furnished clothing for more than 150 fashion shows not only in Elko but also in Wells, Carlin and Battle Mountain. They were sponsored by various organizations as fundraising

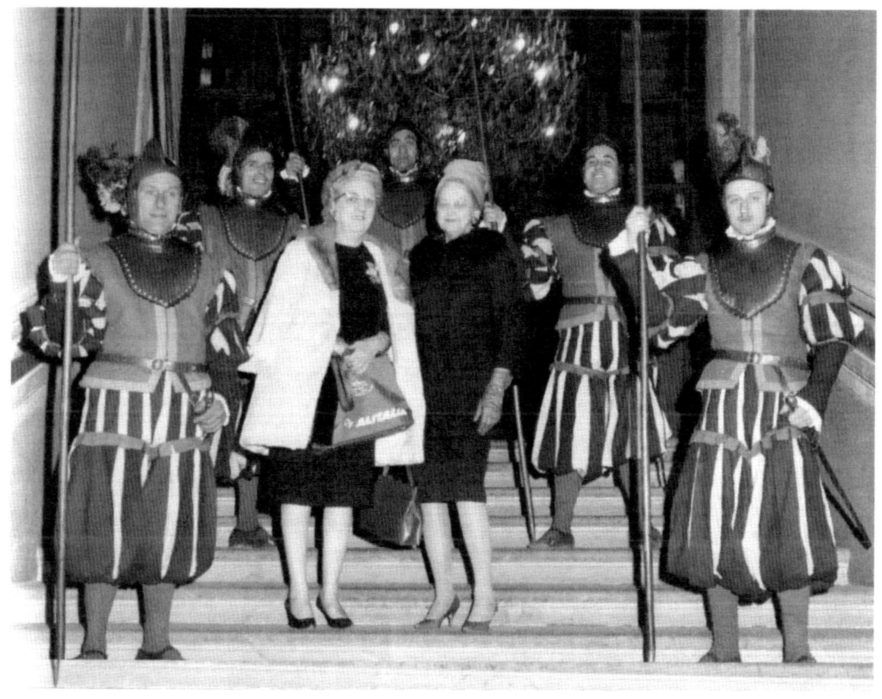

Lillian (*right*) and an unidentified friend sightseeing during a buying trip to Florence, Italy. *Courtesy of Northeastern Nevada Museum.*

events for their groups. She belonged to a number of service organizations and served as an officer in most of them.

She trained many young women who worked for her through the years. She not only taught them all facets of the dress retail business but also passed along her commitment to honest business practices and her interest and participation in public and community affairs. Many of these employees went on to engage in similar enterprises.

During an interview for a news story in the *Elko Daily Free Press*, Lillian said:

> *The best years of my life have been devoted to merchandising.* [They were] *long days, seven days a week. There have been bank failures, lean depression years, long cold winters when no one shopped, 52 degrees below zero one year. Faithful customers, hard-working sales ladies, and quality merchandise have contributed to my success. I love my work. I have dedicated my life to it.*

In 1986, Lillian sold her store after thirty-six years in business. It was resold several times in the next few years. Finally, the doors were closed for a final time in 1996. Lillian Hansen died on September 29, 1994.

The reputation of Lillian's dress shop was an ambassador for Elko in communities all over Nevada, Utah and Idaho. The boxes and bags carrying her distinctive logo have traveled to many corners of the world.

29

J.J. Hylton

From Rags to Riches and Back Again

John Jessie Hylton's entrance into Elko County was anything but impressive. No one who saw him in those days gave him much of a chance at a successful life.

He was born on August 22, 1854, in Norton County, Virginia. The Hyltons were farmers, but they didn't like to stay in one place for long. They had moved four times before J.J., as he preferred to be called, was twenty years old. By then, he was looking for his own adventure and decided to go west. He had heard of gold in California, and with all his possessions in one small bag, he headed out, alone, on horseback to follow his dreams. When he got to Denver, he got a job cutting railroad ties and sold his horse to send the money home to his family.

His job took him to Salt Lake City, where he worked for a while, but soon the job ended. There he was, no job, no horse and no money, but he still wanted to go to California, so he started walking. He walked to Elko, some two hundred miles to the west; it took him several months.

When he finally got to Elko, he looked for another job to earn money to continue on, but jobs were scarce then. He convinced the owner of a restaurant to let him work for his supper for a few days.

He heard of a small town, about thirty-five miles south of Elko, called Skelton, in Mound Valley. The area is now known as Jiggs. There were a few ranches around the little town. With his farming background, he thought there might be work for him, so he headed out, again on foot.

After a hard day of walking, he came to Edgar Reinhart's ranch at South Fork. Reinhart was feeding his hogs, and J.J., who was not only tired but also thirsty, asked Reinhart for a drink of the buttermilk he was giving to his hogs. Reinhart refused, so J.J. didn't even bother to ask for a job.

The next morning, J.J. came to a ranch owned by L.R. "Old Broadhorns" Bradley, who also happened to be the governor of Nevada. Bradley was in Carson City, and the foreman was nowhere to be found. J.J. decided to wait around, which took several days, but when the foreman did reappear, he thought J.J. was a vagrant and told him to move on.

The next ranch was owned by Ted Carville, who would later become the eighteenth governor of Nevada. He also turned J.J. away.

Finally, the next rancher he encountered hired him. Charlie Adams, an old bachelor, agreed to pay J.J. twenty-five dollars a month if he would help with the irrigation and putting up the hay. J.J. was such good help that Carville and Governor Bradley's foreman realized the mistake they had made and tried to hire him away from Charlie. Adams was very conservative with his money, so everyone was surprised when he offered J.J. fifty dollars a month to stay.

Charlie Adams kept his money hidden in various places around the ranch. One day, by accident, J.J. discovered an old carpetbag full of gold coins, so Charlie hid them in the bottom of a flour canister in the kitchen. J.J. helped Charlie with the cooking, and so he stumbled on the gold coins again. Charlie told J.J., "Dammit, you're the snoopiest bird! Can't keep nothin' hid from you." Even though he gave J.J. a hard time, Charlie liked him and kept him on the payroll for the next ten years.

By then J.J. had saved enough money to buy a ranch of his own and enough sheep to get him started in the ranching business. His new place was just down the road from Charlie's ranch.

Now a prosperous rancher, J.J. married Lena Garrecht in October 1889. This was just months before the beginning of the worst winter in Elko County history. Like every other rancher in the area, J.J. suffered huge losses. Although he had moved his sheep herds south to White Pine County, where the winters were usually milder, he lost all twenty-eight hundred head.

Many ranchers went broke and never recovered from that winter, but J.J. managed to buy 250 head to restock. He also decided to diversify and purchased an additional ranch and some cattle. He continued to prosper, adding more ranches and animals to his vast holdings, until he was one of the largest landowners in Elko County. One of the ranches he bought was the Edgar Reinhart ranch, from the man who had refused him a drink of buttermilk years before.

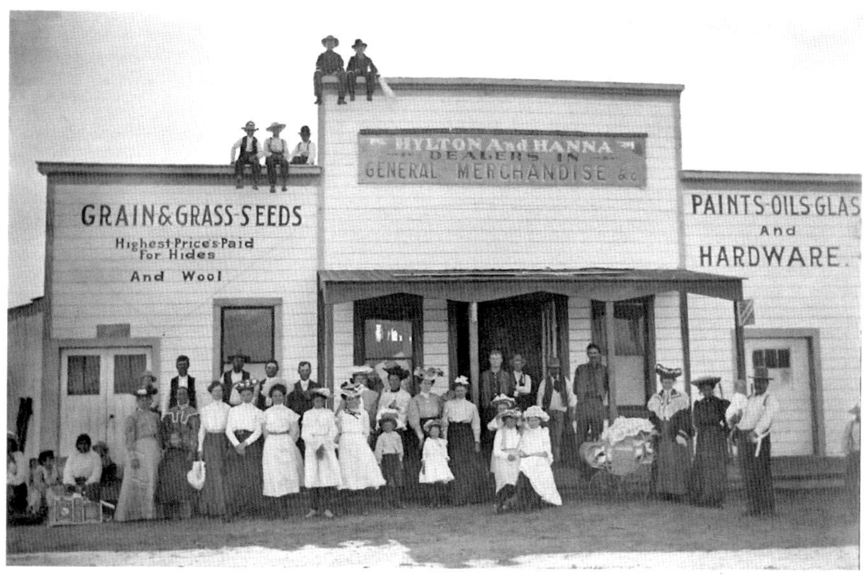

The Hylton and Hanna store in Jiggs, owned by J.J. Hylton and his brother-in-law George Hanna. *Courtesy of Northeastern Nevada Museum.*

J.J. also opened a general merchandise store in Skelton that carried groceries, grains and everything in between. He convinced his brother-in-law George Hanna to move from Texas to Skelton and run the store for him. He changed its name to the Hylton and Hanna store.

J.J. purchased one of the first automobiles in the county when they became available. He apparently managed to handle it fairly well, except one day when he and his wife were driving down a street in Elko and were supposed to stop for lunch at the Commercial Hotel. He just kept driving around in circles, until Lena asked why he was doing that. His reply: "I forgot how to stop the damn thing!"

He built a telephone line from Elko to his store and became a partner in a telephone line to Tuscarora. He also owned two flour mills. J.J. and Lena had two children: a daughter, Jessie, and a son, Lee. J.J. was a good neighbor and was well liked by everyone who knew him.

His prosperity came to an end when the Great Depression hit. The bank forced him into bankruptcy, and he only managed to save a house they had bought in Elko, where they lived the rest of their lives. Lee continued ranching, and Jessie married Archie Dewar, who served as Elko County commissioner for many years. She was an accomplished artist, and her work is prized by local collectors. Archie and Jessie were some of the early,

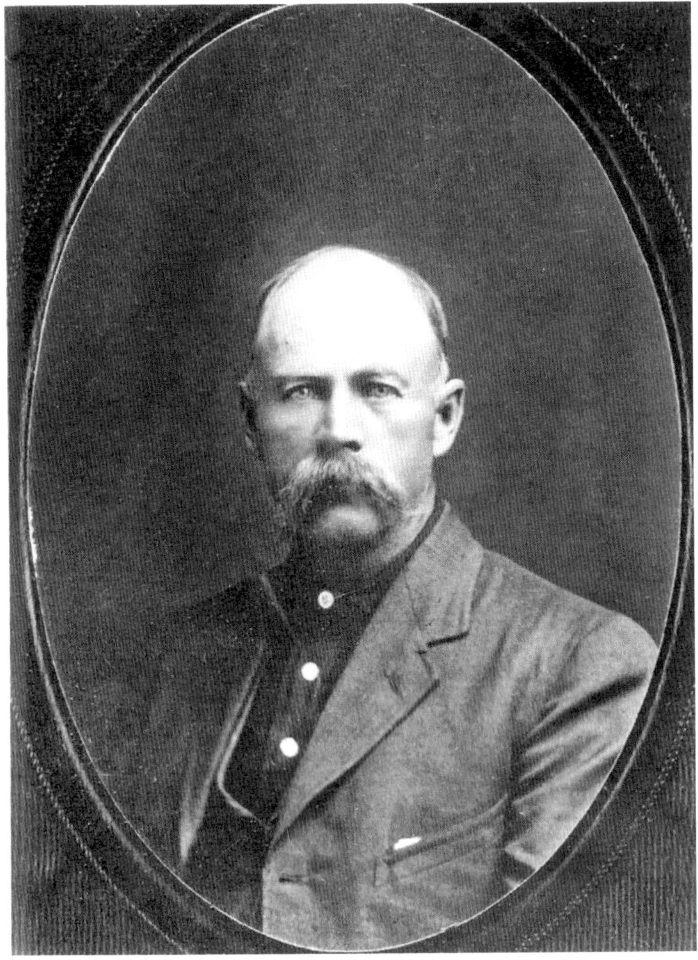

John Jesse "J.J." Hylton. *Courtesy of Northeastern Nevada Museum.*

generous contributors to the Northeastern Nevada Museum in Elko when it was built in 1966.

John Jessie Hylton died in 1947, and Lena Garrecht Hylton passed away in 1950. Neither Jessie nor Lee had any children, so there are no Hylton descendants in Elko County.

30

Oscar Woolverton Griswold

He Never Forgot Where He Came From

Three-star general Oscar Woolverton Griswold might have been one of the best-known, most effective commanders in the U.S. military during two world wars, but he never forgot where he came from. His beginning was quite humble. He was born in a sod shack in Ruby Valley, Nevada, in 1886. It was miles from a city, a hospital, a doctor or much of anything else.

He attended a small rural school in Ruby Valley, then Elko High School and the University of Nevada for one year. He received an appointment to and graduated from the United States Military Academy at West Point in 1910. He was the first Elko County graduate of the academy, and all of Elko County was justifiably proud of him.

He served in World War I and World War II, rising through the ranks and achieving a promotion to lieutenant general in 1945 before retiring in 1947.

During his long, impressive career, he always kept an eye open for men under his command who were from northeastern Nevada. He would invite them to his office, wherever it was, and usually scared them to death in the process. Many didn't know where he was from and had no idea why they were being summoned to the big man's presence. They soon relaxed, though, as he showed them a sprig of sagebrush that his mother sent to him and let them enjoy the familiar fragrance that all real Nevadans love. The men would chat for several hours about cattle, snow, range conditions, rainbow trout and sage hens.

On one occasion, General Griswold heard that one of his soldiers was from Nevada and a fellow West Point graduate. Norvin Davis, a young lieutenant

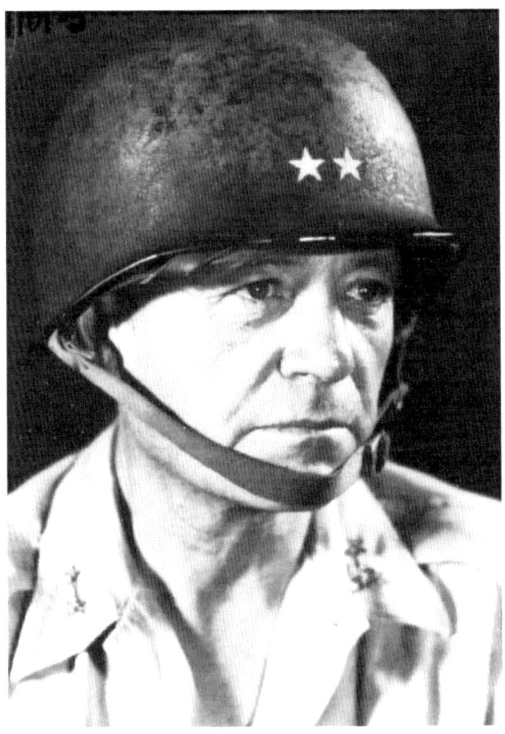

General Oscar Griswold during World War II. *Courtesy of Northeastern Nevada Museum.*

from Wells, only a few miles from where Griswold was born, was understandably nervous when he was told to report to the general's tent. He, too, was soon put at ease as they talked of home. Tragically, young Davis was killed in action during the Battle of Luzon, Philippine Islands, shortly after this visit. General Griswold wrote a personal letter to his parents and ended it with the words, "My hope is those quiet Nevada mountains and open spaces may combine with time to soften and make more bearable your great loss."

Another encounter involved Major Francis Smyth from Beowawe. The general's office was a tent in the middle of the jungle with the sides rolled up. The only furnishings were a desk, a folding chair and a filing cabinet. The general was in plain view of anyone within a hundred yards. Smyth said it had been years since Griswold had ridden the ranges of Elko County as a young man, but he had forgotten little. He asked many questions about the people and conditions in northeastern Nevada and was very interested in how the war was affecting folks back home. They talked for a long time, and Smyth later recounted that he had met a true American hero that day.

Oscar served on the Western Front in France, on the staff of General Pershing during World War I. During that time, he was promoted to first lieutenant, captain, major and then lieutenant colonel. He received a Purple Heart for wounds he received there.

After the war, Oscar was an instructor at both Syracuse University and West Point. The army recognized that he had a great mind for military strategy and decided to send him for more training, which he received at the Army Command & General Staff College and the Army War College.

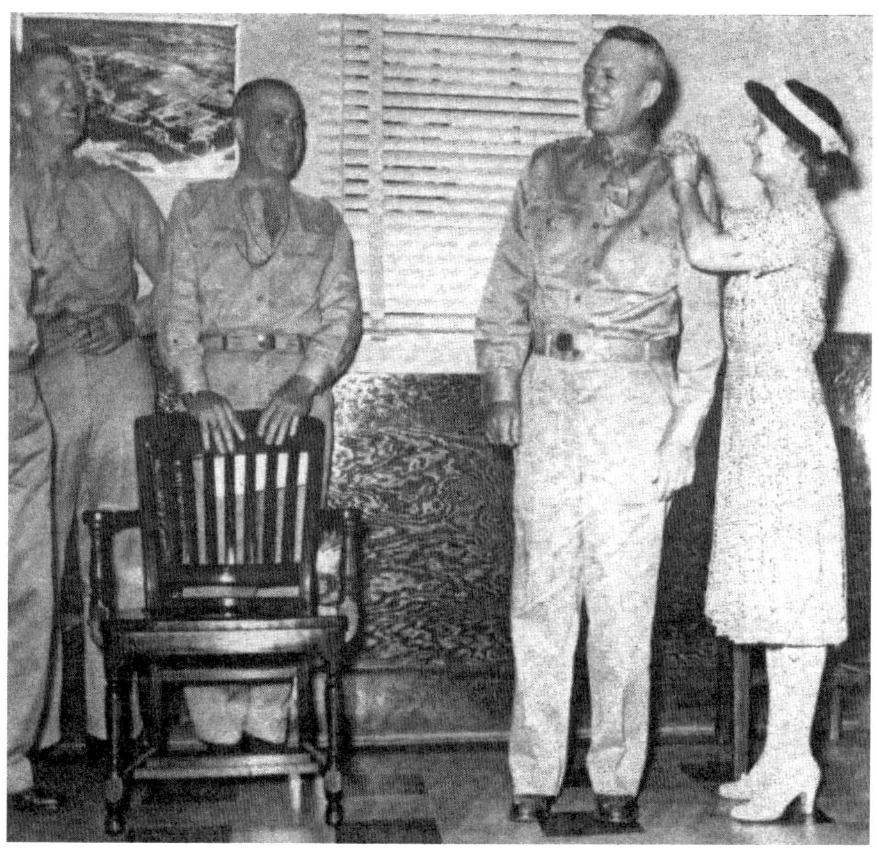

Betty Griswold pinning a medal on her husband, Oscar Griswold. *Courtesy of Northeastern Nevada Museum.*

In 1940, Oscar was promoted to brigadier general and, less than a year later, was promoted to major general.

During World War II, he took command of the XIV Corps and led his troops into battle at Guadalcanal, New Georgia, Bougainville, Green Islands and Emirau Islands. Because of the dense jungles in these areas, the usual attack and defense tactics were useless. Oscar's ability to adapt, show flexibility and develop new strategies was invaluable to the success of these battles.

He established a reputation as a "soldier for soldiers" and a man who greatly valued a strong relationship with his men. At one point during the battle at Bougainville, things were not going well, and Oscar joined the troops in their foxholes. Word quickly spread: "'The Boss is here, we're going to be okay." Within a few days, conditions improved, and the Americans were victorious.

After the war, Oscar and the XIV Corps were part of the occupation force in Japan. He realized how important it was to build a new understanding with the young people of Japan. "The young generation," he said, "must be thoroughly educated in democratic ways before any real progress is made toward a new Japan." He led his troops in teaching democracy to the same people they had been fighting to the death a month earlier. This would have been a difficult task for any commander, but the faith his troops had in him made this possible.

Oscar later wrote a military manual that dealt with leadership situations officers would encounter during their service. The United States Military Academy made it required reading for all cadets.

General Oscar Griswold died in 1959 at the age of seventy-three, twelve years after his retirement. A local newspaper, the *Elko Independent*, in reporting his death, called him the county's most illustrious native. And he never forgot where he came from.

31

ANNA WISEMAN CORYELL

The Silver Coffeepot

Anna Wiseman was born in Wells in 1867 and would live there her entire life.

Horace H. Coryell was born in Illinois in 1852 and became an orphan at a young age. Not much is known of his early life except that, at age seventeen, he came west with a railroad shipment of mules from Missouri. He eventually ended up in Wells.

In 1887, Horace Coryell married Anna Wiseman. He was thirty-five and she was twenty. She was also his biggest supporter.

During the next forty-two years, Horace owned a ranch, was the local bank president, was both a school and church trustee and served a term as grand chancellor of the Knights of Pythias of Nevada. Most impressive, he served for twenty years in the Nevada state legislature as a state senator from Elko County, from 1888 to 1918.

In 1913, while Horace was serving in the Nevada State Senate, he and Anna celebrated their twenty-sixth wedding anniversary. His fellow senators realized that it was also the twenty-sixth session of the legislature, so they thought it called for a celebration. They put their money together and bought the Coryells a silver tea service. It was inscribed:

To Mr. and Mrs. Horace Coryell
From the Nevada Senate
26th Session
26th Anniversary

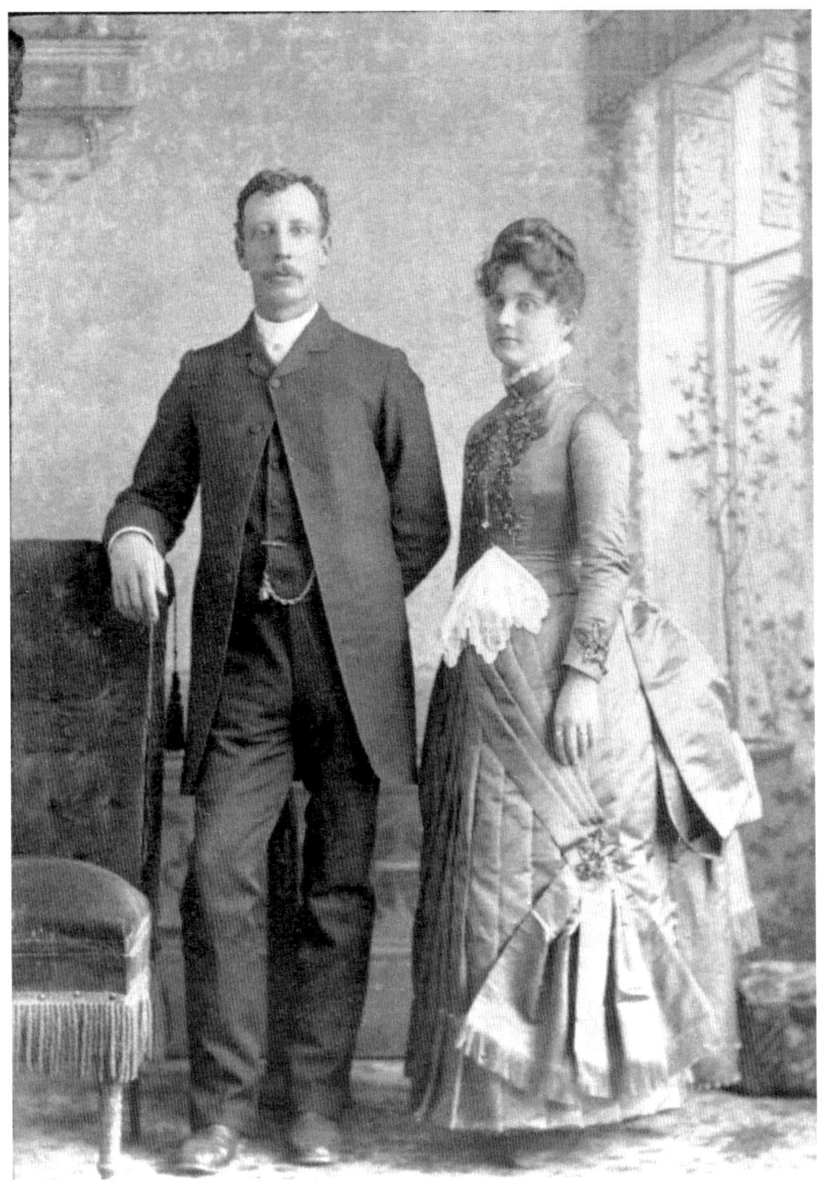

Horace and Anna Coryell on their wedding day, 1887. *Courtesy of Northeastern Nevada Museum.*

Anna was very proud of it, but she didn't like to polish it. Unfortunately, it needed a great deal of polishing. Instead, she put it away in the back of an old china closet.

After Horace retired from the senate, he returned to Wells and became the first mayor of the new town. That career would not last long, as he died in 1928, halfway through his first term. He was seventy-seven. Anna remained in Wells.

In 1930, a big disagreement developed among the citizens of Wells. There was already a small school building, only twenty years old, but the town had grown and the school was bursting at the seams. The kindergartners had to meet in the basement, which was not a pleasant place. The floors and walls were concrete, and the few windows were high up on the walls, but it was during the Great Depression, and money was scarce. However, the city leaders put a $75,000 school bond on the ballot for the upcoming election in May, and the arguments were on.

The members of the Commercial Club, a local women's group, were in favor of the new school and decided to hold a banquet to feed all the town citizens and try to convince them, while they were well fed and happy, to vote for the bond.

Anna Coryell was not a member of the Commercial Club, but she decided to do her part, so she polished up the coffeepot from the silver service and took it to be used during the banquet.

The dinner was a big success, with nearly everyone in town attending. There were plenty of arguments about the school bond during the evening. Younger people who had kids in school wanted it, and most of the older folks were dead-set against it.

Harry Tuttle did a good portion of the talking. Always outspoken, he owned a lot of taxable property and could see his taxes rising. He made an impassioned plea for defeating the bond issue. He didn't feel bad about the kindergartners in the basement, he explained, because back in his day, they didn't send kids to school before they were out of their cradles. He said he wasn't against education, but Wells

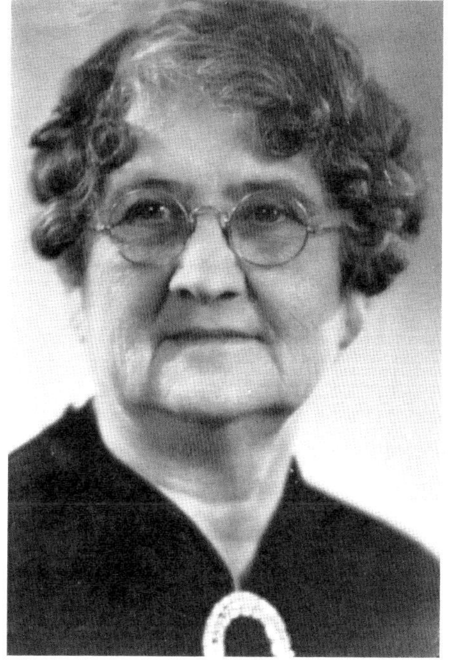

Anna Coryell. *Courtesy of Northeastern Nevada Museum.*

already had a grammar school, and "it was time somebody told those young yahoos that money doesn't grow on every damn sagebrush." Harry was well respected in town, and many people agreed with him.

Another problem cropped up during the banquet. There was an old heating stove in the back room used to keep the coffeepots warm. As one of the ladies reached for a new, hot pot to fill cups, she saw little bright beads of melted silver bouncing around the other pots that were warming there. The culprit was a silver pot someone had carelessly put back on the stove when it was empty, and it had melted one of the legs and burned the bottom black. Of course, it was the coffeepot from the Nevada Senate silver set. She hurriedly took it off the stove, put it in a coal bucket and pushed it behind the stove.

Anna Coryell was not aware of what had happened. At the next Commercial Club meeting, the ladies discussed getting the coffeepot repaired. It was going to cost them fourteen dollars, a lot of money in those days. Some of them didn't want to do it; some said Anna should not have brought such a valuable thing to the dinner; but a few of them insisted that they must do it, so it was sent off to be fixed. No one ever wondered why Anna Coryell didn't ask about her coffeepot or question why she didn't have it back.

Meanwhile, the day of the election arrived. Those in favor of the bond managed to have the election held in the dark, dreary basement of the old school. Several of the men went so far as to replace the few lights bulbs that hung from the ceiling with ten-watt bulbs, so there would be even less light.

Harry Tuttle was the first one at the polls that morning. At that time, he was still opposed to the bond. After trying to vote in the dim conditions, he blustered out of the voting booth, his ballot unmarked, and went over by one of the high windows for more light. After that, he headed downtown and told everyone who would listen that the kids couldn't learn in those conditions and that they needed a new school. The bond issue passed by a large margin.

Meanwhile, the coffeepot came back from the repair shop. It looked beautiful. The grumblers, now happy the bond issue had passed, were also happy about the coffeepot. A group of women went to Anna Coryell's house to return the pot. They were surprised by her reaction when she said, "I ought to have you arrested." She wasn't laughing. "Now you've gone and had the coffeepot polished, I'll have to shine the rest of that silver."

32

Joe Billy and Julia Smith

A Hearty Dozen

Joe Billy and Julia Smith were ordinary ranchers in Ruby Valley most of their lives, similar to many other couples in the 1800s. Except for one amazing thing.

They had twelve children. That wasn't at all unusual in those days. The unusual thing was, they all lived to adulthood and all died of old age. It would have been more commonplace, then, for many of them to die as babies and more as youngsters or teenagers or even young adults. Most couples who had that many children only ended up with a few surviving into old age.

Joseph William Smith was born in Lehi, Utah, in 1852. He went by Joe Billy his entire life. His parents were both born in England and traveled to America with their parents when they were young children. They met and married in White Cloud, Missouri, and traveled west with a group of pioneers in 1850 and settled in Lehi. They would have fourteen children, but most of them died at a young age. Joe Billy was the oldest.

One day after their ninth child was born, Joe Billy's father took his team and wagon to Salt Lake City, fifty miles north of Lehi, to get supplies. Along the way, he saw a comely woman standing by the road and offered her a ride, and when they arrived in Salt Lake City, they were married. Polygamy was fairly common in Utah at that time, but it was customary for a man to at least get his other wife's permission before marrying someone else. He neglected to do this. When he brought his new wife home, wife number one refused to let her in the house, so he had to secure another place for her to live.

Joe Billy did not take kindly to this new wife, either, because he saw how much pain it caused his mother. The last straw was when his father insisted Joe Billy help the new wife with her chores. He knew people from Lehi who had settled in Ruby Valley, Nevada, and was sure he could find a job with them, so at age seventeen he decided to leave home. He gathered a few things and set out for Ruby Valley, taking only a horse, bedroll, shotgun, flour, bacon and coffee. He knew he could kill jackrabbits to eat along the way. According to a crude map he had of the area, it was about 250 miles. He knew if he avoided the dangerous salt flats, he could make it. His horse went lame after three days, so he walked the rest of the way. It took him nearly a month, but he found a good job when he got there.

He worked on ranches for a few years until he had saved enough money to buy a team and wagon and started freighting. He hauled grain, turkeys, chickens and eggs from Ruby Valley to Eureka, two hundred miles southwest,

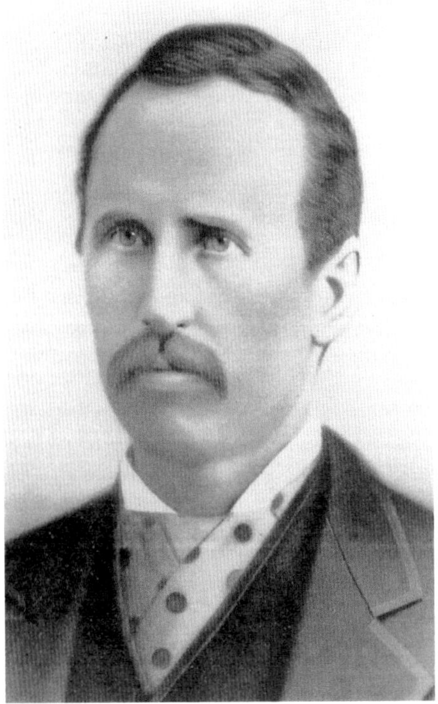

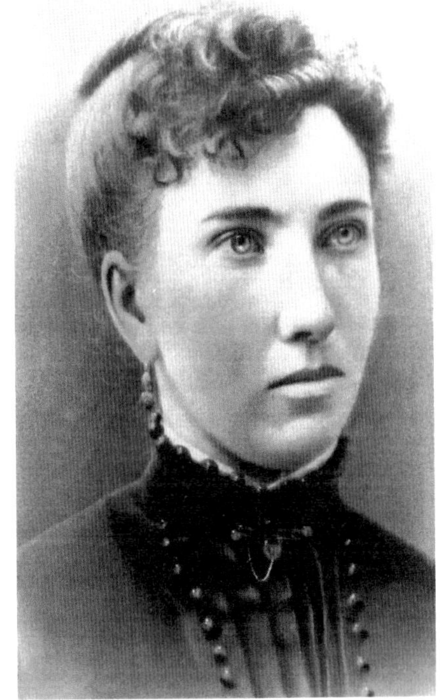

Left: Joseph William "Joe Billy" Smith on his wedding day. *Courtesy of Northeastern Nevada Museum.*

Right: Julie McCracken Smith on her wedding day. *Courtesy of Northeastern Nevada Museum.*

and sold them to people working in the big silver mines. It took him three weeks to get to the mining camps and three weeks back, but he built up a prosperous business. He eventually acquired more wagons and teams to pull them. He finally saved enough to buy a ranch in Ruby Valley. He decided it was time to get married.

He traveled back to Lehi and, while attending a dance, was taken with a young lady, Julia Ann McCracken. She was born in Provo, Utah, in 1867, but her father died when she was six years old, and her mother died when she was twelve. She was an only child and an orphan at a young age; she had had a hard life up to that point. After the dance, Joe Billy went back to Ruby Valley, but the couple corresponded for several years.

They were married in 1885, and she moved to the ranch in Ruby Valley. Joe Billy was thirty-three and Julia was eighteen. Because she had never had a family, she was determined to have a big one, and they had twelve children. The first one was born in Utah, at the home of Joe Billy's parents. The next eight were born in Ruby Valley, with neighboring women assisting as midwives. The tenth baby came in the middle of a blizzard—Joe Billy had

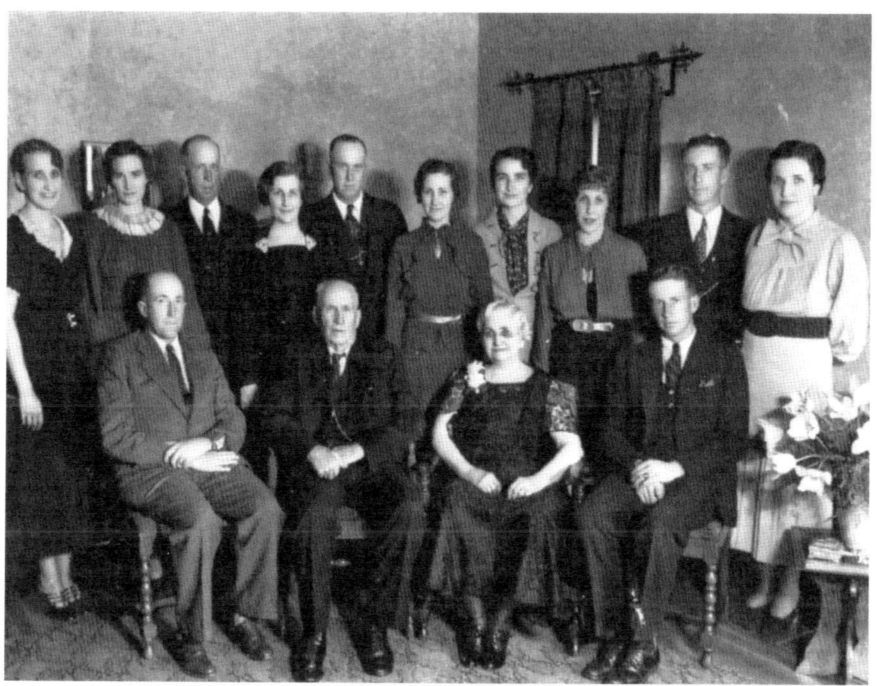

Joe Billy and Julia Smith (*seated, center*) on their fiftieth wedding anniversary in 1935, with their twelve children. *Courtesy of Northeastern Nevada Museum.*

to be the doctor, nurse and midwife. He vowed that this would not happen again, so Julia stayed in town for the births of the last two.

The children attended school in Ruby Valley until the oldest one became high school age, at which point Joe Billy bought a large house in Salt Lake City. Julia and the children would move there during the school year and then come back to the ranch in the summer. Joe Billy traveled by train to Salt Lake City to spend Christmas holidays with his family, and he would always take a live turkey in a sack with him. The train conductor usually put up a big fuss about that, but Joe Billy always won the argument.

Many changes occurred during Joe Billy and Julia's lifetime. When they were young, they saw pioneers come into Utah in ox-drawn wagons with handmade farm implements. They watched as electricity, telephones, automobiles, radios, airplanes and television became commonplace. Joe Billy saw his first movie in Salt Lake City when he was eighty-four years old.

Joe Billy died in 1940, at age eighty-eight, and Julia passed away in 1943, at age seventy-six. The death of their first child was in 1957, at age fifty-four, and the last of their children died in 2004, at age ninety-one.

33

JESS RANKER

A Man of Manly Bearing and Good Common Sense

Jess Ranker was going to be an attorney, but a little mining town in Nevada named Tuscarora changed his mind.

Jess grew up on a ranch in California and graduated from Chico State Normal School with a two-year degree. He excelled in everything he did there. In addition to getting good grades, he was the captain of the baseball, basketball and football teams and was in charge of military training. He was also on the boxing team, which would turn out to be very useful to him in Tuscarora a few years later.

Jess's plan was to continue in school and study law. One day, near the end of his time in Chico, while walking home, he passed a teacher's placement agency and stopped to take a look. The manager spotted him, and they started visiting. By the time the conversation was over, Jess had signed up to be the principal and teacher in a small school in Tuscarora. He wasn't especially thrilled about the school part, but hunting and fishing in the area really caught his attention.

In the fall of 1910, he boarded a train for Nevada. When he arrived in Elko, the only way to Tuscarora was by stagecoach, drawn by four horses over fifty-two miles of dirt road. An adventuresome type, he took it all in stride.

His new job was to be the principal of the school and teach the seventh, eighth and ninth grades. His contract was for ten months, $100 per month. He taught all subjects.

Jess had no teaching experience, but he felt secure because he had several books that told him how to teach. One of them was *Bagley's School Room*

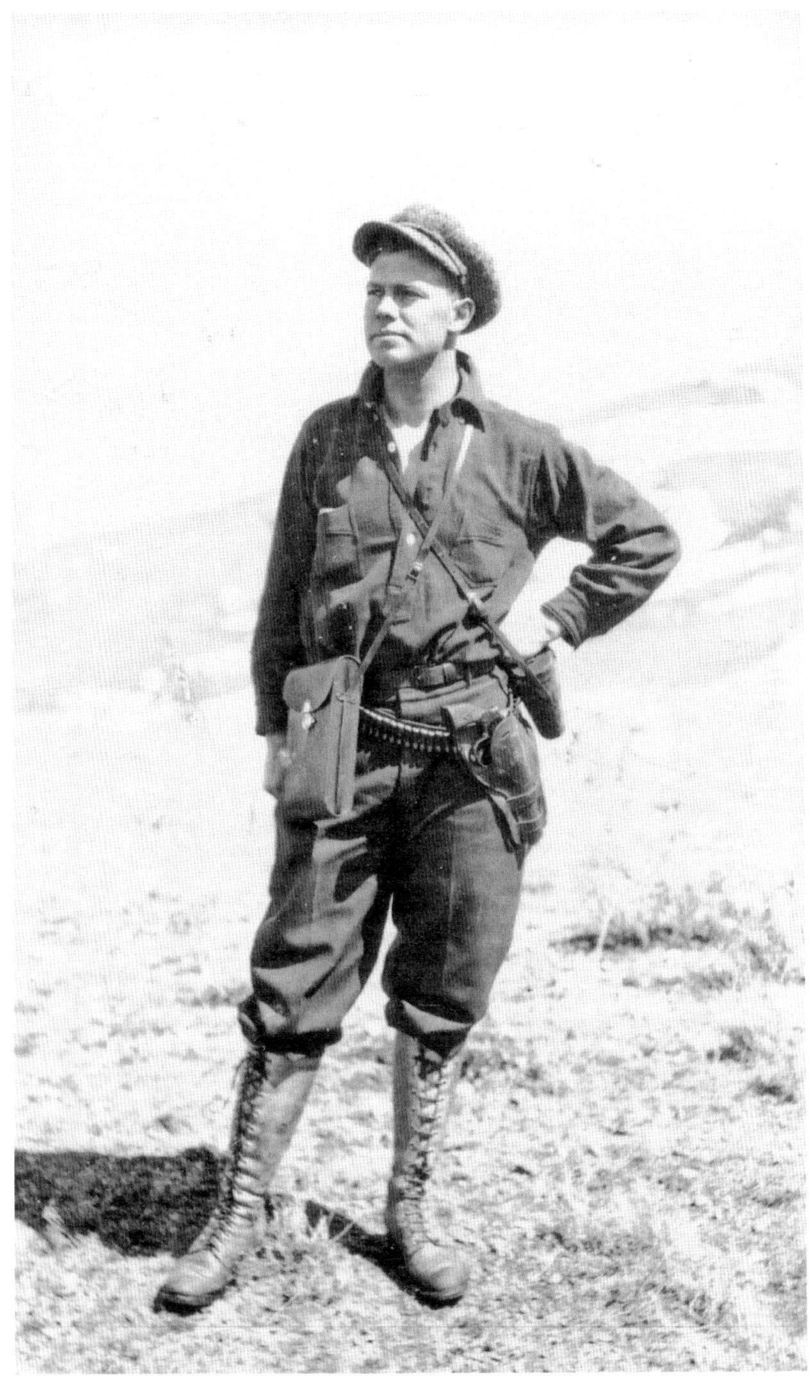

Jess Ranker walking around Tuscarora. *Courtesy of Northeastern Nevada Museum.*

Management. It only took a couple of weeks to realize that the methods in the books didn't always work and that common sense and humor did work. He never had any discipline problems.

There were about thirty-five to forty kids in Tuscarora and two school buildings for nine grades. Older students boarded in Elko to attend high school.

Tuscarora had long since passed the boom years of the 1870s, and there were only about five hundred people left in town, down from the more than three thousand in earlier years. All of the mines were shut down except for the Dexter mine, which was still operating. Most buildings were either boarded up or falling down, and Jess lived in a building called a hotel, but it was not much more than a nearly abandoned shack. The mining equipment, left abandoned when miners had moved on to the next bonanza, sat there, rusting away.

Jess became intrigued with the mining business. Because he didn't realize how dangerous it could be, he started poking around in old, abandoned mine shafts. Most of the large timbers that had been used to shore up the tunnels were gone by this time. Timbers were very expensive, because they had to be shipped from California, so when a mine played out, they were removed and used elsewhere. With no timbers left, cave-ins were a constant danger. Jess didn't have a miner's lamp, so he used candles, but this was actually a good thing. When his candle started to flicker and the flame became small, he knew enough to realize the oxygen was getting scarce, and he would back out of that tunnel. Finally, some of the townspeople realized what he was doing and persuaded him to stop his dangerous explorations.

He soon became friends with the hoist engineer of the Dexter, who would take him down in the mine so he could look around. The shaft went straight down, with tunnels going out about every fifty feet. He spent much of his free time exploring there.

Like most of the rural areas of the time, people had to provide their own entertainment. There was a town hall with a cantilevered floor that could be tipped to a slant when a play was presented and then moved flat for dancing. Jess soon had a group of friends and liked to have a drink with them on occasion. He had his whiskey sent from Reno, as he thought the liquor served at the local saloon was more like ink.

Jess was popular with the students and parents alike, but occasionally they tried to test him to see what he was made of. A group of men held boxing matches in the back room of one of the saloons, and they invited him to join in. One of them wondered out loud if "the Prof" (as he was called) would like to put on the gloves and go a few rounds. Because of his previous experience, he had some fun with the situation. He toyed with his opponent in the beginning and then got a few good licks in. The other man, feeling frustrated, charged after Jess like a mad bull and soon found himself on the losing end of things. The Prof gained a good deal of respect with the local miners that night.

Cowboys on local ranches would occasionally come to town. On one such occasion, Jess was standing near the bar when a cowboy wondered, out loud, who the dude in the fancy clothes was. When told he was a teacher, the drunk cowboy wondered if the teacher knew how to dance. He started shooting his pistol near Jess's feet; Jess remained cool and just stood and looked at him. No fun at all!

Another time, after too much whiskey, a cowboy got on his horse and promptly got bucked off. Jess saw it happen and laughed. The cowboy challenged him to try and ride it, which he did. He then told the cowboy that, now that the horse was broke, it was safe to ride him. The kids had all watched it happen, and Jess was rapidly becoming their hero. People soon learned they shouldn't underestimate him. He could do just about anything that came along.

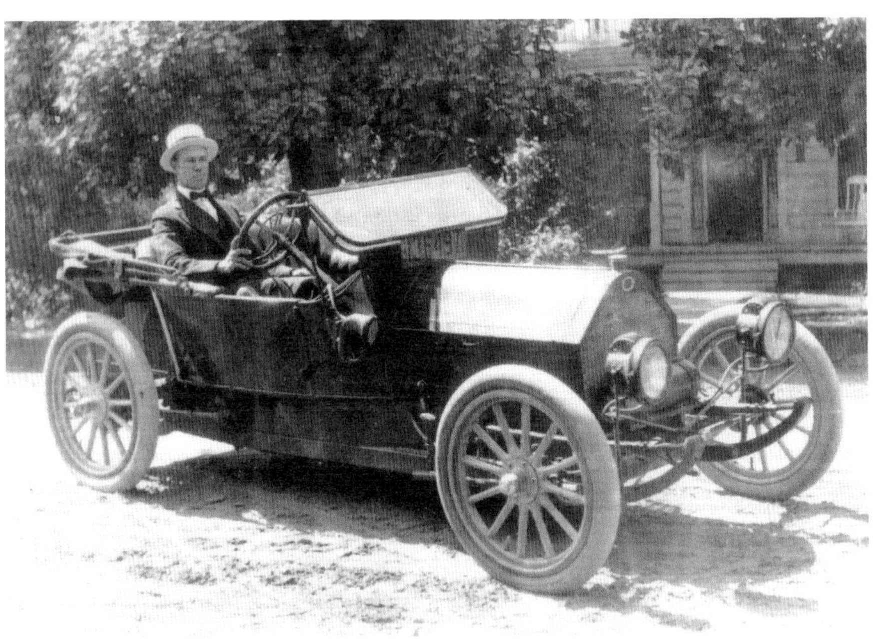

Jess Ranker in his new automobile, driving in Tuscarora. *Courtesy of Northeastern Nevada Museum.*

In the spring, Jess organized a baseball team, and he was one of the best players. When he left town for summer vacation, the team wrote to him, imploring him to return because they weren't much good without him. They told him they had a game on Labor Day with a team from Owyhee and were sure to get clobbered if he didn't come back.

Jess courted Irene Tuttle most of the time he was in Tuscarora. She had gone to school in Tuscarora and was teaching in another school six miles away. Jess thought she was a nice girl but apparently was not in love with her, because after two years, he decided to leave Tuscarora without her. He returned to California and taught school in several places for the next forty-one years, retiring in Alhambra, California.

A letter of recommendation he received from the school board as he left Tuscarora stated, "He is a young man of manly bearing and pleasing address. His refinement and natural good common sense enables him to adapt himself to any social requirements. We recommended him to any school board that desires a lively, manly, efficient principal for their school."

34

Aaron Ross

Not on My Watch

Aaron Y. Ross had a reputation as a tough man to deal with, but the train robbers didn't know that, or know that he was guarding the Wells Fargo shipment in January 1883.

Many tales are told of stagecoach holdups in the area, but train robberies were not very common, as the railroad had only been built through Elko County some fourteen years earlier.

On this fateful day, a Central Pacific train, headed east, approached the small town of Montello, in northeastern Elko County. The engineer noticed a flashing red light on the water tank. As this was unusual, he stopped his train. As he stepped out of the cab to see what was going on, two masked men grabbed him and shoved him in the tank house, where he joined the conductor, brakeman and fireman, who had been escorted there by other desperados. After the train crew was securely bound, hand and foot, the would-be robbers approached the Wells Fargo & Company express car and pounded on the door, demanding that it be opened. Aaron Ross, who was guarding the contents, opened the door a crack and found himself looking down the barrel of a revolver.

Aaron had been in this sort of predicament before, and he always came out ahead. While driving a stagecoach in Montana sixteen years earlier, twenty-five Indians attacked him. After he killed five of them, the rest decided the attack was not a good idea and left. Again in Montana, ten years later, he killed the outlaw "Big Jack" Davis during a failed stagecoach robbery. Wells Fargo had already given him a $650 gold watch for his exploits on its behalf. Needless to say, the robbers in Montello had no idea what they were up against.

Aaron slammed and latched the door. They yelled at him to open the door, and he told them to wait while he put his boots on. "Never mind your boots," an outlaw shouted. "You can put them on after we get through with you."

Aaron ignored them and fired several shots through the side of the car, in the direction the shouting was coming from. That quieted them down for a while, but then they threatened to set the boxcar on fire and murder him if he didn't open the door. He still refused. The men then positioned themselves on all four corners of the car and shot into the middle of it. Aaron was hit three times: once on his finger, once on his hip and a third near his watch pocket. The robbers climbed up to uncouple the car. Aaron shot twice more and somehow managed to wound three of them.

Suddenly, a No. 2 westbound express whistle sounded. The outlaws grabbed the engineer, untied him and forced him to back the train onto a siding. They stopped No. 2, pointed a gun at the engineer and told him to move on. He did.

Then they returned to the Wells Fargo car, retrieved the brakeman from the shed and forced him at gunpoint to uncouple the cars. Then, changing their minds, they attempted to break through the door of Aaron's car with a pickaxe. He stayed out of the way and waited. That was not successful, so they ordered the engineer to back the train up and ram the express car. The impact forced the door to spring open, but Aaron quickly closed and latched it. They again forced the engineer to back into the car, and again the door sprung open. Aaron closed and latched it again. They tried the engine a third time, but it was nearly out of steam and didn't hit hard

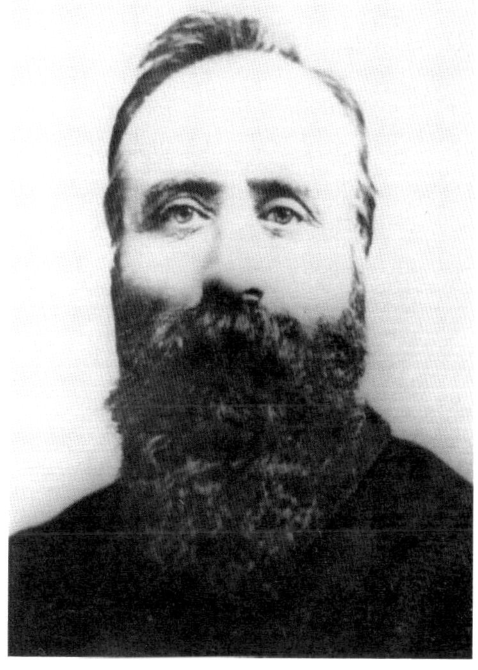

Aaron Y. Ross. *Courtesy of Northeastern Nevada Museum.*

enough to open the door. Next, they went looking for wood to start a fire to smoke Aaron out, but finding none, the frustrated outlaws gave up and rode away, with only ten dollars they had taken from the conductor's pocket.

Sheriff Henry Taber from Elko organized a posse, and with the help of Utah law enforcement, the would-be robbers were apprehended near Delta, Utah, several days later.

Aaron Ross was not through with them, however. The prisoners were on the train, headed to Elko to face prosecution, when it stopped in Montello and Aaron boarded. He was also headed to Elko to testify against them in court.

One of the outlaws, Frank Francis, and Aaron discovered that they were acquaintances from years earlier. They were pleasant to each other and talked about old times during the journey.

The outlaws spent a few years in the Nevada State Penitentiary, and Aaron Ross, for his bravery and quick wit, received $1,000 from Wells Fargo. He died in 1922 at the age of ninety-three. His obituary appeared in the *New York Times*.

Bibliography

Bowman, Nora Linger. *Only the Mountains Remain*. Caldwell, ID: Caxton Printers, 1958.

Butterfield, Roger. *Life* magazine. April 18, 1949.

Carlson, Helen S. *Nevada Place Names: A Geographical Dictionary*. Reno: University of Nevada Press, 1974.

Elko Daily Free Press. Elko, NV.

Elko Independent. Elko, NV.

Haws, Adelaid. *The Valley of Tall Grass*. Caldwell, ID: Caxton Printers, 1950.

McElrath, Jean. *Aged in Sage*. Wells, NV: 1964.

———. *Tumbleweeds by Jean, 1940–1967*. Wells, NV: 1971.

Myles, Myrtle Tate. *Nevada's Governors: From Territorial Days to the Present, 1861–1971*. Sparks, NV: Western Printing & Publishing Company, 1972.

Nevada State Journal. Reno, NV.

Patterson, Edna B., Louise A. Ulph and Victor Goodwin. *Nevada's Northeast Frontier*. Sparks, NV: Western Printing & Publishing Company, 1969.

Quarterlies. Northeastern Nevada Historical Society & Museum. Elko, NV: 1971–2016.

Sweeney, Les. Interview. Payette, ID.

Truett, Velma Stevens. *On the Hoof in Nevada*. Los Angeles: Gehrett-Truett-Hall, 1950.

White Pine News. Ely, NV.

Index

About the Author

Claudia Dahl Wines was raised on a ranch in Elko County and has lived on ranches most of her life.

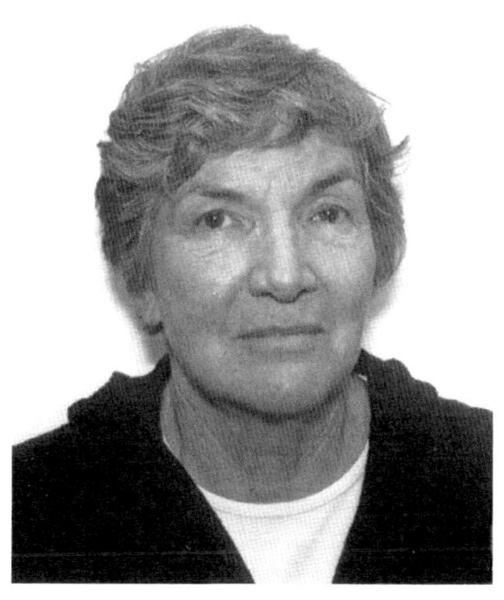

She taught school for many years, both elementary and high school. She served as the editor of two company newsletters at a large gold mine in Elko County and recently retired as executive director of the Northeastern Nevada Museum in Elko, a position she held for fourteen years.

Claudia was married to the late Gordon Wines, a rancher, and has four children, three children-in-law and seven grandchildren.

Her hobbies are reading, historical research, gardening, sewing and needlework.